CAPACITY

Create Laser Focus, Boundless Energy, and an Unstoppable Drive in Any Organization

Chris Johnson
Matt Johnson

WILEY

Published by John Wiley & Sons, Inc., Hoboken, New Jersey.
Published simultaneously in Canada.

For general information about our other products and services, please contact our Customer Care Department within the United States at (800) 762-2974, outside the United States at (317) 572-3993 or fax (317) 572-4002.

Wiley publishes in a variety of print and electronic formats and by print-on-demand. Some material included with standard print versions of this book may not be included in e-books or in print-on-demand. If this book refers to media such as a CD or DVD that is not included in the version you purchased, you may download this material at http://booksupport.wiley.com. For more information about Wiley products, visit www.wiley.com.

Library of Congress Cataloging-in-Publication Data:

Names: Johnson, Chris, 1957- author. | Johnson, Matt, 1986- author.
Title: Capacity : create laser focus, boundless energy, and an unstoppable
    drive in any organization / by Chris Johnson, Matt Johnson.
Description: Hoboken, New Jersey : John Wiley & Sons, Inc., [2018] | Includes
    index. |
Identifiers: LCCN 2017044991 (print) | LCCN 2017051278 (ebook) | ISBN
    9781119387381 (pdf) | ISBN 9781119387282 (epub) | ISBN 9781119386971
    (cloth)
Subjects: LCSH: Organizational effectiveness. | Performance. | Organizational
    change. | Organizational behavior.
Classification: LCC HD58.9 (ebook) | LCC HD58.9 .J637 2018 (print) | DDC
    658.3/14–dc23
LC record available at https://lccn.loc.gov/2017044991

Printed in the United States of America

10 9 8 7 6 5 4 3 2 1

To the future.
And to Eze, who inspires us to build capacity!

Contents

Introduction: Into the Future

Pause for a moment and reflect on your station in life. How did you end up where you are now? Each of us follows a different path to the present, and we are never quite sure what the future holds. Our journeys through life are paved with hard work, luck, and a handful of critical moments. But if you really think about it, what influenced your work ethic and opportunities the most? As much as we like to think that we alone determine our outcomes in life, it's simply not the case.

Despite everything we do to forge our own identities, we are all destined to become a little, or a lot, like our parents. Author Neil Postman once wrote that children are "the living messages we send to a time we will not see."[1] That realization may still be unsettling for a lot of us, but instead of fighting the inevitable, let's embrace it.

Just look at your family tree. Go back three generations. It's safe to say that your great-grandfather toiled away in a factory or field for a tiny fraction of your current salary. Some may not consider his life much of a success. But like every parent before and after him, his definition of a fulfilled life wasn't measured by material wealth, social status, or even his own welfare. He was driven by an innate desire we all share—to help create a better world for his children and the next generation.

Survival does not fuel ambition. Game-changing ideas don't revolutionize the world without a fundamental belief that we can build a better future. That unwavering faith in the promise of tomorrow is the ultimate cure for the human condition.

[1] Postman, Neil. (1982) *The Disappearance of Childhood.* Delacorte Press, NY.

We all want the same thing—whether you are a millennial or baby boomer. We want to leave a lasting legacy to honor those we love most and to inspire those to come. We are all daughters and sons trying to live up to our parents' examples. So, let me tell you a story about my father and why he inspires me.

My father, Chris Johnson (coauthor of this book), took an unorthodox route to success. While attending Western Michigan University from 1976 to 1980, he spent each summer working either at the assembly line at Oldsmobile or in construction. After graduating with a degree in business and economics, and filling out hundreds of applications for job openings, he still had not landed the dream job to which he aspired. The economy in Michigan was extremely soft, so he went back to Oldsmobile, installing bumpers for an entire year. With car sales dipping well below profitable projections, he and dozens of his colleagues were laid off. Despite the sudden upheaval, he didn't waste any time pounding the pavement for his next gig. After a couple of months, he was hired by Butternut Bread as a route salesperson, delivering white bread and Dolly Madison cakes and cupcakes. His workday was certainly not a piece of cake! It was a grueling, sleep-deprived, 80-plus-hour-a-week job that started around 2:30 a.m. and ended around 5:00 p.m. After a year of grinding it out with Butternut Bread, Dad went to work for Frito-Lay—delivering Doritos, Ruffles, Cheetos, Munchos, and Funyons as a route salesperson. Frito-Lay was a much better job, with normal hours and the opportunity for advancement. After a year with Frito-Lay, he knew this type of work wasn't his calling and would never challenge him to be the best version of himself. He decided to go back to graduate school at Michigan State University in the exercise physiology program. During his first semester, his wife Paula (my mom) announced she was pregnant, and a few months later they found out they were going to have twins. He spent the next four years working full time for Frito-Lay, raising his new twins, and finishing his graduate degree from Michigan State University. He always had a passion for health and fitness and soon found his gift to share with the world: being the prevention guy!

Dad went to work for a hospital-based wellness center after receiving his master's degree. Early on he was recruited by Dr. Barry Saltman, a family practice physician, to help design and implement a training facility for high-risk patients. This group was littered with all types of chronic illness—diabetes, morbid obesity, chronic obstructive pulmonary disease (COPD), cancer, and heart disease, just to name a few. If patients had an extreme health problem or were on the verge of irreversible damage, they were sent to the Well Aware Health and Fitness Center to work with my dad. These life-altering experiences forged a wealth of knowledge in the health and fitness space that built the foundation for his successful future.

In 1990, Dad was chosen to pioneer a personal training program for the Michigan Athletic Club, one of the largest hospital-based health clubs in the world. This program went on to become one of

Chris with his family: wife Paula, twins Matt and Kristen.

the world's first million-dollar personal training programs. During his 16 years at the Michigan Athletic Club, he authored four books and created his signature Food Target program. He has coached over 20,000 hours of individual training and has given keynote addresses to over 500,000 people. In 2006, he launched On Target Living, a health and performance company that works with organizations around the globe. He is the epitome of walking the walk when it comes to self-improvement and has truly changed thousands of lives for the better.

I have learned a lot from my dad, but hands down the most valuable lesson from my dad is how to be curious: "Ask better questions and you'll get better answers." That mantra has guided him through seemingly insurmountable adversity. We want you to be curious while you read this book. Ask the tough questions and strive to see if there is a better way. Dad wasn't the smartest or most talented, but boundless curiosity and hard work paved his road to success. I have met a lot of different people with exemplary talents and abilities, and one thing is for certain—I've never seen or met someone with more capacity than my father! Thirty years ago, he didn't intentionally say, "I must expand my capacity"; he just did it.

Searching for Success

Before explaining what capacity is and why it's needed, let's talk about something everyone is chasing and probably thinking about right now: success. We all want *success*.

However, we all define success differently. Some of us just want a high-paying job or to introduce a profitable product. Many of us want to forge meaningful relationships and raise well-rounded children. However you define success, you want to look back on your legacy and smile.

If success is what we crave, then failure is what we avoid. Failure hurts. Failure is scary, yet it's the best way to create meaningful change. Failure shapes us into the people we want to be. J. K. Rowling was unemployed and depressed when she finally finished Harry Potter. Michael Jordan was cut from his varsity basketball team, and Abraham Lincoln failed at countless ventures before becoming president. The foundation of this book was built on the lessons learned from overcoming failure.

Every article or video on success seems to unlock a magical secret to attaining it. It is very interesting to watch people search for this one easy trick. They seem to play whack-a-mole with various schemes, without any clear process or plan for applying new strategies to their own lives. Is it possible that we are overlooking part of the equation? Are we overthinking a simple process? Is there even a process at all?

Like in martial arts, in life there is a fundamental truth we can't avoid: Most of us start as white belts. Maybe some start as green belts, but nobody starts as a black belt. Every dojo is built on the foundational belief that there's no one true way to achieve the highest level of mastery. You must ultimately build your capacity—emotionally, physically, and psychologically. We will show you exactly how to do this. We know you want to be successful. We know you want to have a successful organization. Capacity is the secret to success; the organizations and people with the largest capacity always perform better in the long run.

1 The Secret That Is Overlooked

Capacity is the ability to use every skill and resource at your disposal.

—Dr. Phil Nuernberger,
author Strong and Fearless

We believe this book can be the catalyst for our two most insatiable desires: *success* and *happiness*.

Every leader and organization recognizes the power of professional development and skills training. Without evolving people, processes, and products, organizations will not survive changing demands and fierce competition. Without growth, market share begins to erode until there's no bottom line left to protect. And yet, despite heavy investment in ongoing development, most organizations fail to see the kind of cultural transformation they desperately want. The road to transformation is littered with the carcasses of once-great giants who spent millions upon millions on professional development. Employee engagement is at an all-time low. Productivity is decreasing rapidly with endless e-mails, meetings, and electronic distractions diminishing focus, stifling creativity, and slaughtering innovation.

Look around your office—is this the best it can be? What can your organization do to thrive and prosper? What if it were possible to improve the organization one person, one team, and one leader at a time—not by simply teaching more or turning up the volume, but by plugging into a deeper source?

Our capacity for change is limitless. Our ancestors have shown us what's possible if we all unite under the universal theme of human progress—creating a better future built on an expanded capacity for change. We are a resilient species that plows the fields of failure in order to plant the seeds of change. We will show you how to capture the hearts and minds of your people and provide a clear, compelling, and actionable path toward transformation and prolonged prosperity. It's time to look inward and unleash your full potential.

What Is Capacity?

We have all used the word *capacity* in our daily lives to describe maximal storage or effort. What's the towing capacity of my pickup truck? What's my lung capacity? Let's look at the formal definition of capacity:

ca·pac·i·ty

1. The maximum amount that something can contain
2. The ability or power to do, experience, or understand something

Here is how we want you to think about capacity:

- Capacity is the ability to do more, the ability to have more, and the ability to give more.
- As you increase your capacity, you increase your ability to do more with seemingly less.
- Everyone has unused potential energy waiting to be converted to purposeful action.

There is no question that some people are simply born with more talent or skills than others. One of the hallmarks of a fully realized life is optimizing your innate abilities and applying them with maximum efficiency. We have all witnessed the often-tragic

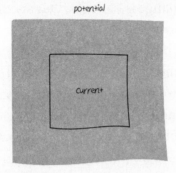

FIGURE 1.1 Expanding your container. We must all expand our containers.

trajectories of child protégés. They were destined for stardom and had every conceivable advantage to pave a surefire road to glory. Then out of nowhere, a lesser talent makes a bigger impact than the protégé ever dreamed! This book isn't about the merits of talent over training or taking shortcuts to success. *Capacity* is about asking the tough questions that lead to better choices and expanding your body's ability to contain more input without sacrificing the quality of your body's output (Figure 1.1).

What follows is a list of a few names you might recognize. There is no question that all of these people have talent—in many cases a ton of talent—but we think you would all agree there are graveyards full of talented people with unrealized aspirations and dreams.

Sara Blakely, founder and owner of SPANX

"It all started with a pair of pantyhose, some scissors, and a bright idea." Sara cut the feet out of her pantyhose to make her butt look better in white pants. To start this dream, she saved $5,000 by selling fax machines. From there she spent all of the money submitting a patent she wrote herself while practically begging hundreds of manufacturers to produce the first prototype. Don't underestimate a woman with fanatic focus on changing other women's lives! Sara had to push her capacity to create success.

Arianna Huffington, cofounder and editor-in-chief of *The Huffington Post*

Recently, Arianna wrote a book titled *The Sleep Revolution* about her journey to renewing her relationship with sleep. She had a paradigm shift after she fainted from exhaustion and hit her head on her desk, breaking her chin bone and requiring five stitches on her eye. At this point in her career, people thought of Arianna as a super-talented, highly successful media mogul, but she wasn't at her best. She discovered that sleep allowed her to be more productive, more inspired, and more joyful in life. She expanded her capacity through sleep.

LeBron James, five-time NBA MVP

"The King" was born with generational talent for the game of basketball. He skyrocketed from the streets of Akron, Ohio, to the front cover of *Sports Illustrated* by his seventeenth birthday. Unlike many stars before him, LeBron knew he couldn't rely on talent alone to be considered one of the best players to ever lace it up. He adheres to a strict routine of clean eating, mindfulness training, yoga, rest, and recovery to ensure he has more than enough gas in the tank for a grueling NBA season.

Chesley Sullenberger, American Airlines captain

During an emergency, Chesley "Sully" Sullenberger landed Flight 1549 on the Hudson River—saving all 155 people aboard! Captain Sully flew fighters in the military before he started flying commercial airliners. He also flew gliders during his downtime, which have zero propulsion. There was no mandate from the airline to cross-train with different types of aircraft. His passion for pure flight created the capacity to gently land a 70-ton behemoth with complete engine failure (Figure 1.2). He may have been the only person capable of that landing. As he has said:

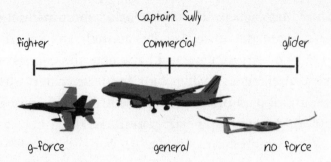

FIGURE 1.2 Captain Sully's experience.

The way I describe this whole experience—is that everything I had done in my career had in some way been a preparation for that moment. There were probably some things that were more important than others or that applied more directly. But I felt like everything I'd done in some way contributed to the outcome—of course along with [the actions of] my first officer and the flight attendant crew, the cooperative behavior of the passengers during the evacuation, and the prompt and efficient response of the first responders in New York.[1]

Tom Brady, five-time Super Bowl–winning quarterback

He was drafted in the sixth round of the 2000 NFL draft. Brady was the 199th overall selection in the draft that year, and as crazy as it sounds, was the sixth quarterback to be selected that year—the *sixth*! How could seasoned scouts, coaches, and general managers of these highly sophisticated professional football franchises all miss such a talented athlete? Did Tom Brady not have the talent these football experts were looking for? Tom Brady had talent—maybe he did not possess the unrefined talent that other quarterbacks selected ahead of him had in abundance—but there is no mistaking that Brady had talent! What separates Brady from many other talented athletes is his desire to get better through a systematic process

[1] https://www.airspacemag.com/as-interview/aamps-interview-sullys-tale-53584029/

to build his capacity. His off-the-field conditioning and nutritional regimen is unrivaled. His aptitude and mastery of the system devised by his coach, arguably the greatest football coach of all time, enables him to thrive under unrelenting pressure and punishment from elite NFL defenses. Brady built his capacity for greater performance.

■ ■ ■

Think of all the talented people who fell short in life. Many just relied on their talent and skill, without growing their capacity to do more with it. Now think of the seemingly talentless person who changed the world by consistently growing their capacity and refusing to settle for less.

What Tom Brady, LeBron James, Captain Sully, Arianna Huffington, and Sara Blakely possess—what separates talented athletes, people, and organizations—is the desire for continuous improvement. These folks build a rock-solid foundation and carefully construct a process of incremental improvements on top of it.

Resilience is a common attribute used to describe countless people who have shaped our world for the better. Here is something to think about—the definition of resilience is the *capacity* to recover quickly from adversity or strife. Toughness is the great equalizer. Some people are born with natural abilities, talents, and skills, but capacity must be earned and managed.

Most Successful People and Organizations Have Two Things in Common

First, you must develop a growth mindset—small incremental steps for continuous improvement without succumbing to the arrogance and complacency of immediate success.

Second, nobody starts out being great—they all slowly build their ability to be great. Everyone has similar raw materials, but the game changer for almost everyone is the ability to build capacity.

We are at our best when we are growing and learning so we can accomplish the seemingly impossible! Growth is the most rewarding part of a fully realized life!

There are many books on the secrets and shortcuts to success. These can be very entertaining and a great way to provoke new thoughts and shatter preconceived notions, but no amount of new ideas will come to fruition without working hard. Building capacity is not easy. You never took shortcuts to achieve all you have up to this point and neither should a system that sustains it.

Here are just a few shortcuts we hear and see every day:

- Get rich quick
- Take an energy drink to increase energy
- Lose weight without exercise
- Improve IQ without learning
- Take a magic pill and heal
- Enhance sex drive without building relationships
- Hire talent to be the best organization

Many organizations and their people may lose hope over time and give up. This can happen for multiple reasons, but if you boil it down, in most cases it comes down to losing capacity!

- Capacity to focus
- Capacity to lead
- Capacity to innovate
- Capacity to create
- Capacity to learn
- Capacity to grow
- Capacity to think
- Capacity to breathe
- Capacity to move
- Capacity to love

Do you feel like your organization and your people are expanding their capacity? Changing behavior can be extremely difficult, and it begins with self-awareness.

Ask yourself, "How much am I willing to devote to improving my skills and increasing my capacity for greatness?" "How much time is my organization spending on increasing capacity?" If you resolve to put in the hard work and follow a process through despite all obstacles, you will prevail over any challenge.

Here are a few questions to ask before embarking on this journey:

Organizational Capacity

1. Does your team feel or perform like they are overwhelmed?
2. Is stress a noticeable problem throughout your culture?
3. Have you had cutting-edge innovation in the last 3, 6, or 12 months?
4. Is there sustainable and profitable revenue growth?
5. Are you giving back to charities or the community?
6. Is your organization the number-one source of positive influence in your employees' lives?

Individual Capacity

1. Are you currently learning something new?
2. Do you have clear focus on your purpose?
3. On a scale of 1–10, is your energy level 8.5 or higher most days, hours, and minutes?
4. Do you have time for family, friends, or volunteering?
5. Does the thought of doing more upset or frustrate you?
6. Do you feel you are fulfilling your purpose?

Now that we've done a little soul-searching, it's time to get started. There are thousands of self-help books, consultants, and programs on how to accelerate growth, innovate, and increase profit margins. Many organizations and their people are doing tremendous work. The real key to thriving in today's economy is making better choices about building an inexhaustible supply of energy to tackle any problem in the most efficient way.

We can't simply upload the extra capacity and push play. Humans aren't built like machines. Human capacity must be learned, practiced, and developed. It all starts with changing the mindset of organizations from the top down to create and sustain unstoppable growth fueled by healthier and happier people. Albert Einstein once stated, "The true sign of intelligence is not knowledge, but imagination." Intelligence and performance are really two sides to the same coin. Imagine the possibilities if we all had greater capacity to accomplish more without having to learn a new skill or language. We only need to focus our attention inward before we can radiate greatness outward.

Capacity is your secret weapon to winning the performance war.

Key Point

Capacity is your ability to *do more*, *have more*, and *give more*. This is your container; imagine if you had more room!

2 People with a Purpose

Recently I (Matt) was invited to speak at the annual retreat for a large CPA firm. As I was sitting in the back and waiting to present to the partners, I listened as the president addressed the group. He spent 30 minutes going over the objectives for the three-day retreat. This was a typical retreat designed to help organizations to align, strengthen, and communicate the direction the organization is taking to move forward into the future.

Before I speak to any group, I make sure to interview the organizers, meeting planners, and executive team to tap into what outcomes they want from my presentation and consulting. The tough part is transparency. We usually get the superficial answer that sounds great, but we often fail to hear the exact pain points and initiatives of the entire organization. At the CPA firm retreat it was different, and it was as clear what obstacles were in the way.

The president discussed all the challenges and obstacles. Retention and talent were the unanimous front runners. Staff engagement wasn't far behind, and the common dialogue of how to work with millennials and the next generation was something on their minds. Retention and talent were so important that I remember one slide that included the word *retention* five times. The consistent theme was that many of the struggles and opportunities centered on people. I didn't hear much discussion of technology, systems, computers, or software.

As I was getting closer to my time, I was wondering, "Do they know that these are the outcomes we help drive? Do they know these challenges are what every organization has? Are they going to do what every organization is doing or are they going to think differently?"

This was the perfect setup; they were already talking about the problems they were having and were desperate to find a strategic solution. Little did they know these are the problems I mention to start off my presentation, and I was going to give them the solutions.

It was now my turn.

I started with "Isn't every organization trying to be better just like you?" They all laughed and agreed—yes, this is an obvious statement. From there I asked, "What is the definition of an organization?

Now they looked at me with the look of someone who has already heard this message, but it wasn't going to be the same message; it wasn't going to be the same solution. I was going to go at the source of the problem and to do that, you must ask better questions!

"So, if we are trying to become better as an organization, let's first look at the definition of an organization:"

or·gan·i·za·tion
noun
1. an organized body of *people* with a particular *purpose*, especially a business, society, association, etc.

It's simple. All organizations are *people with a purpose*.

My next statement was "So, if I asked you what is the most valuable asset of your organization, what would you say?"

The entire room said *people*. I have never had an organization or leader tell me that people are not their number-one asset. If this is the universal answer, the next question we need to ask is, "What is the most valuable asset of your people?"

The entire room went quiet when I asked this question. Nobody wanted to shout out an answer; you could tell they didn't get this far yet.

I said, "It is their *health*; your people's most valuable asset is their health. To build the best organization you must build the most valuable asset of your most valuable asset."

You could see the bomb go off in their heads; it is so simple, so obvious, but so far from the direction most organizations are going. To expand capacity of your people or organization it is essential to build foundational health.

1. What is the most valuable asset of your organization? What would you say? *Our people*
2. What is the most valuable asset of your people? What would you say? *Their health*
3. To build the best organization you must build the most valuable asset of your most valuable asset.

You may be thinking, "Another wellness book, another book on a soft skill, another book on something else we need to do." After you read this book you will realize this isn't just another thing to do; this isn't a soft skill that has unmeasurable ROI, and this is not a wellness book. This book was designed after 30 years of work helping *people* perform at their best; this book was created to shift the thinking to help organizations unlock their true capacity, their true potential.

This book will not have all the answers or solutions to your problems and opportunities. What this book is designed to do is to allow you to think differently about the future of your people and your organization. Simply, this is the foundational blueprint to building the most optimized person and culture to fulfill your established purpose. This book is one of the first written by a baby boomer and a millennial to help all generations and all organizations improve the one thing that will always matter: *people*.

Our definition of healthy is to be your most optimized self. Without comparing you to others or peers, we can help you optimize the gifts, talents, and attributes you have.

Not a Priority

It was late spring of 2009, I (Matt) had just completed my last round as a college golfer for Grand Valley State University. I graduated with a major in corporate fitness/wellness and a minor in entrepreneurial business. I knew what I wanted to do. I had always known I wanted to help organizations be better by improving the health of their people, but I really didn't know what this career path looked like.

Maybe my passion started when I was 14 or 15, riding in the car with my twin sister and Dad to and from school, listening to the audio version of the famous business book *Good to Great* by Jim Collins. Now don't get me wrong, this was extremely boring at the time and I would have much rather listened to music on the radio, but I still remember being fascinated with organizational structures and the growth and scale these organizations could have.

Dad is an amazing mentor. He is a health guru who has consulted thousands of people and hundreds of organizations. He devoted his life to helping individuals be healthier, and he created his company along the way called On Target Living.

At this point after college I was blessed to have unique experience in the world of health, but where could I make the biggest difference? During college, I watched as my dad would travel the globe speaking and training organizations and their people, so it was promising that there was this desire out there for organizations to get their people healthier. This is what I saw as my opportunity or biggest impact—helping organizations improve the health of their people.

My first jumping-off point came when I had a breakfast meeting with the CEO of a Fortune 500 company. He was interested in meeting with me because health-care costs were going up, and he could tell the health and performance of his people were going down. He thought it would be wise to create a wellness program for the company's 5,000 employees. This seemed to be right in my wheelhouse—a chance to help people inside a large organization. I was ready to blast off, but there was one slowdown: The CEO wanted me to learn the business before I could create a health and wellness strategy. I agreed and was eager to learn.

Things were going great; I was working and learning how the company functioned, and I received amazing skill training on industry communication, Outlook, Excel, business writing, workflow, customer service, and teamwork. The only problem was that I wasn't doing what I loved: helping people get better and be their best. So, I would intermittently continue the dialogue with the CEO: "When can I create this wellness strategy?" The answer would always be the same: "I think it is important, but not a priority right now." So, I just continued to do my work and built some wonderful relationships with my workmates.

As I continued asking, I kept hitting the same roadblock: "We think it would be nice, but it isn't a priority." I wanted to emphasize that I was extremely grateful for what this company provided me, but I knew there was a better way. The health-care costs and the health of the people were not going in the direction they should or could. Although the company's financial success and growth looked good on paper, I knew that it could be so much better. People could have been happier; their energy could have been higher; they didn't have to suffer through their pain and disease. I think they had a lot more potential.

Not long after that, I was presented with an opportunity to work at On Target Living with my dad. On Target Living had grown to a point where Dad needed help scaling, managing, and creating new programs, so I made the leap. Again, my recent experience with this Fortune 500 company was a great jumping-off point in my career. It triggered questions on why and how to get organizations to want to be healthier.

When I started my new position at On Target Living, I thought it would be fulfilling, challenging, and extremely rewarding. Boy, did I have a lot to learn. I was right about one thing—the challenge. It felt sometimes like I was pulling teeth. When I approached organizations about their wellness plans, I kept hearing the same thing I heard at my past company: "Yes, we are interested, yes we have these challenges, but it isn't a priority right now" or "We don't have a budget for this." Mind you many of the organizations we were speaking with were multimillion- or multibillion-dollar organizations—hence, they had plenty of money.

We would have fantastic success with groups of employees; then we would arrange a meeting with the senior leadership, HR departments, and benefits people to create a strategy, and they would tell us all their challenges. Prescription drug costs are high, people are low on energy, morale is down, engagement is lousy, obesity is running wild, and stress is out of control. We would say, "We can help. We can help make your organization *healthier*." (Remember this statement, because up until now I would lead the conversation with we want to help you with your employee *health* and *wellness*.)

Let's bring our attention back to the *purpose*. Like we pointed out, organizations are *people with a purpose*. Over the last several years the popularity and strategy of communicating one's purpose, mission, and vision are at an all-time high. Studies have shown that people want to fulfill their purpose; people also want to buy from organizations with greater purpose. These organizations are spending millions of dollars creating, communicating, and advertising their purpose. I would say this is not anything new, and most of you know about having a purpose that is communicated to your employees and customers.

So, if we have this purpose thing figured out, why don't we invest in people the same way? That is a much more complicated piece with a lot of moving parts. It's like creating a to do list; it feels good when you can complete something. In regard to purpose, you can complete this task. In regard to people, the work and investment never end.

Attracting talent is a top strategy for almost every organization in the world. Here are the common features of an organization seeking to attract talent:

1. New hundred-million-dollar office building
2. Amazing cafeterias with sushi and executive chefs
3. Big-screen TVs
4. Cutting-edge technology and data
5. Incentives for their people
6. Fitbits, wearable technology, gadgets
7. Ergonomic lighting and desks
8. Lobbies that look like museums

Look around, is this your organization? The ability to offer this is a privilege and will help you attract the best talent and people. This is a fantastic strategy to attract talent, but it will not build talent.

MINDSET SHIFT

The definition of insanity is to do the same thing repeatedly and expecting different results. On Target Living kept running into the same story when meeting with business leaders: We want to be the best organization, we want better performance, we need to get more productivity from our people, and we can't keep

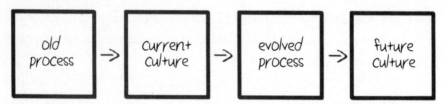

FIGURE 2.1 If you want a different outcome, you must change the process.

paying for this health-care elephant—but they continued to have the mindset that health and wellness were not top priorities and that wellness is not a business strategy. I finally stepped back and said, "What am I missing?" I went back to my Entrepreneurship 101 roots and the first question we learned to ask in my business program: Is there a problem? (Yes.) If so, do you have a solution to fix it? (Yes.) But the decision makers of these organizations didn't want this solution. Even more profound, they didn't believe it was a solution to their problem.

Conclusion: We must ask better questions!

At that point, we had worked with hundreds of companies and thousands of people, and helped improve health outcomes, lower health-care costs, increase engagement, and make the culture healthier. Despite this, we continued to struggle making it a business strategy or solution. Most often it was a one-off, feel-good event, with no strategy or long-term vision.

This was our *aha* moment: It wasn't that the organizations didn't see the value; it wasn't that they didn't agree it helped. The problem? It wasn't truly what they *wanted*; we weren't giving them exactly what they *wanted*.

Over the past 10 years, we have worked with, researched, and studied hundreds of public and private, large and small businesses; government agencies; hospital systems; and military services, and have come up with the question and answer that shifted the mindset and the solution.

What Do All Organizations *Want?*

It is not that this is a novel idea. It isn't an overly sophisticated idea, but it is a paradigm shift in the mindset of how you look at the performance of your people and why you want to look at this different mindset for the future success of your organization.

What every organization is looking for is how to optimize the people they have and the people they will have. It boils down to three performance outcomes.

Focus | Energy | Drive

These three performance outcomes lead to an organization that has the infinite capacity to fulfill its purpose. I didn't say that wrong: an infinite capacity to do what it is your organization is set out to do.

You might be saying, Matt, you have oversimplified what organizations want. My organization wants to increase profitability, secure the happiness of its shareholders or board of directors, develop groundbreaking innovations, have a world-changing impact, and even reduce risks. Those are important and attractive desires, but they won't get you very far.

What we have found is that when you define what an organization is, you start to see why and how *focus, energy,* and *drive* will lead you to become the best organization you are trying to be!

A light bulb went off in my mind when I first read this. It was so simple.

People with a purpose

Every organization—no matter the size, scale, or resources—has a purpose; this is why it exists. This could be to make the best automobile, to make money for the founders' family, to cure cancer, to serve underprivileged people or anything and everything. Every organization has a purpose. The key element is that it is always people who make up this purpose; this is what we hope you take away from this book: how to improve your performance and that of your people to raise the tide of your organization.

If you want to have the most impactful, successful, and innovation organization you must start with the people.

Peter Drucker, considered the founder of modern management, said this so elegantly in his book *Effective Executive*:

> Self-development of the effective executive is central to development of the organization. Whether it is a business, government agency, research laboratory, hospital or military service. It is the way toward performance of the organization. They raise the sights of people—their own as well as others.
>
> Thus, the organization not only becomes capable of doing better. It becomes capable of doing different things and of aspiring to different goals.

Improve the *People*, Improve the Organization

Organizations are just *people with a purpose*, and we are going to show you how to improve your people's most valuable asset—*health*.

Let us walk you through how to help yourorganization create laser focus, boundless energy, and an unstoppable drive to achieve the *purpose* you have set out to fulfill.

Ask yourself: Do organizations want a health strategy, or a strategy that targets their people's focus, energy, and drive?

This was the critical moment; we changed the mindset on performance. Organizations don't connect the dots of health and wellness to performance, but when you say *focus*, *energy*, and *drive*, they want to know when and where to start.

Your most efficient way to become the best organization is to build the best people. If you have a purpose to fulfill, you will always want to build your people first. And start with their number-one asset: *health*.

It is not optional to build your people. If you do, you will succeed; if you don't, you will fail.

We were working with a CEO of a large insurance company; during his tenure the participation in our training was close to 99 percent. We asked him, "How do you get this kind of participation?" He laughed and said, "Because it is important."

If you make something a core part of your strategy, it usually gets noticed. If you make something optional, what is the point of even doing it?

Don't make building your people's health optional; make it a core part of your strategy.

Key Point

All organizations are *people with a purpose*. You must build your most valuable assets' most valuable asset: their health.

3 Drinking from a Firehose Wastes a Lot of Water

The organizational landscape has undergone tectonic shifts in the last 15 years. Despite our exponentially greater connectivity and perceived collaboration, productivity and employee development have remained stagnant. Nearly every organization invests considerable resources toward improvement initiatives. They all want to scale up for growth by improving their workforce. But in the past two years, only 8 percent of business initiatives met all expectations, with $70.6 billion allocated in 2016 alone, up nearly 35 percent since 2013.

Throwing more money at a problem isn't the solution.

What the data tells us is managers and leaders are not being developed the right way. Schedule as many meetings and create as much content as you want—the symptoms of an ailing organizations will still persist.

Organizations need to stop and ask a few critical questions: What is the source of the problem? What are the problems and challenges? If you ask better questions, you tend to get better answers. *How* will your organization need to develop and adapt for the future?

Imagine a 16.9-ounce water bottle filled to the brim (this represents demands). Water is the fuel of life and a perfect representation

FIGURE 3.1 Our cups are overflowing

of the fluid demands of a full life—family, friends, creativity, new ideas, sales projections, meetings, deadlines, hobbies, health, joy, and even happiness. Now the objective is to pour this water bottle into a glass that has the *capacity* of 15 ounces (your capacity). What will the result be? (See Figure 3.1.)

Most of us will pour as much as we can into our glass, hoping the really important stuff doesn't spill over. We might even try to wait for the water in the glass to evaporate so we can squeeze in the last 1.9 ounces. But who are we kidding? You can't just turn off the demands of a full life.

We repeatedly witness this mentality across the organizational spectrum. Most attempt to manage this by adding more layers of information from the top down: "We need more sales training. We need more leadership training. We need better management processes. Our workflow needs streamlining. Let's send out another e-mail explaining the system again. Just keep giving more information!"

What if we all paused and accepted the inconvenient truth: Our people are drowning from the increasing demands. There's tremendous value in prioritizing tasks to work more efficiently, but as you will see shortly, it doesn't address the source of the problem. Having helped hundreds of organizations optimize performance and productivity, we know that asking people to wear more hats and juggle too many tasks usually leads to sloppy work and burned-out employees. If you figure out which hat fits them best and increase their capacity to handle whatever is thrown at them, they will thrive under pressure.

So let's analyze these persistent performance problems more closely.

Top Five Problems

1. Demands are increasing, capacity is shrinking.
2. Stress is melting us down.
3. We over-rely on skills and talent.
4. Engagement is lousy.
5. Our health is embarrassing.

---

1. Demands Are Increasing, Capacity Is Shrinking

We were recently speaking to a state-run government organization. The executive director addressed the staff before we went on stage. She said:

> I want to let you all know that I am expecting a lot from you. In doing so we will be providing all the tools and resources needed to manage this. We are expecting you to do more with less, and to be honest, we will continue to ask more of you.

The common trend across every industry and every organization is to *do more* with *less*.

If you think about it, no species has arguably achieved more, with less innate ability, than humans. If you ask any anthropologist, they will tell you the only superior physical traits we possess are endurance running and a steely digestive tract. Civilization was

Increasing demands, shrinking capacity.

built on the evolution of ideas and their application.

When an organization thinks of doing more, it's in terms of revenue growth, clients served, products made, products created, and general innovation—the collective output of any enterprise. People, time, and money are the input side of the equation. We've been far too fixated on value engineering input, instead of focusing on what produces the best output.

A great example of this is the legendary Palace of Versailles near Paris. It is one of the most marvelous properties in the world and is staggering to comprehend. It was the epicenter of the kingdom of France from 1682 to 1789 when King Louis XIV decided to build and glorify his majesty through unrivaled opulence and splendor. This project took an estimated 50,000 workers over 50 years to build. The sheer magnitude of manpower and dedication is almost impossible to fathom today. The hallmark of modern society is to evolve at an exponential level with less labor, while also producing more capital.

Gordon Moore co-founded Intel in the late 1950s and proposed one of the most radical theories of the twentieth century—Moore's law—which states that computer processing power will double each year until we reach a singular moment where technological productivity will exceed human output (Figure 3.2). Not only can your smartphone process more information than Skylab, but it costs 0.0001 percent the amount of one of the most powerful portable supercomputers of the late 1970s. Moore's law doesn't apply to the human condition, but it's all too evident in today's technological ecosystem.

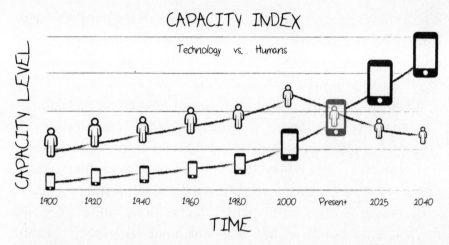

FIGURE 3.2 Human capacity is lagging behind technology.

Our collective focus has been completely obliterated by these new shiny screens that we are forced to interface with every waking moment:

- Our average attention span is eight seconds.
- We send 269 billion e-mails a day; that is up from 215.3 billion in 2016.
- The average smartphone user taps, swipes, or clicks their phone 2,617 times a day.

Not only are companies expected to produce more with less resources, but our brains are expected to process more than they were ever designed to. Just type "distracted driving tests" into YouTube and see what happens when humans try to multitask while driving.

We believe organizations will always want to do more with less, and we believe they can succeed at doing this if they start to look at *how* you build the best human beings instead of buying the best *technology*.

Your people know more information than ever before but rarely have the time or opportunity to apply it. We must teach our people how to build a better container for creative productivity. Capacity is not innate; you need to build it. Some people start with larger capacities, but optimum capacity is shaped and strengthened through better foundational health.

We are always amazed by how the most progressive and enlightened corporate cultures are designed and built. We see basketball courts, Nerf guns in the office, pet-friendly work environments, remote working, flex hours, and even craft beer on tap! But behind closed doors, every executive tells us what we already suspected— performance goals are still falling short. Sure, these amenities may attract better talent, but they don't build better people. Every human wants to learn and wants to grow. People yearn for a self-actualized life that aspires to the best versions of themselves. But what we all need to learn more than ever is how to build capacity, because we are all asked to do more with less.

Every organization wants to drive certain key metrics, whether they be engagement, loyalty, creativity, innovation, hard work, growth, happiness, or health. If you truly want these things, you have to teach your people what they need to know in order to accomplish them. Skills training or the occasional hour-long webinar won't satisfy the unquenchable thirst for enrichment.

Information overload is not learning. Endless webinars, manuals, surveys, and e-mails are only diminishing our attention spans and diminishing our retention levels. If you enlist in the US Air Force and are selected for the pilot training program, you spend weeks learning how to use a firearm in basic training. Then you log thousands of simulated and live flight hours to attain the qualifications to pilot an aircraft. Your drill sergeant doesn't e-mail you a three-page PDF illustrated guide or send you a link to a YouTube video on how to pilot an F-16 that goes 1,300 mph. Doesn't a PDF- and YouTube-based training approach sound woefully inadequate for the performance output expected from our brave and capable service members?

Learning is not absorbing information and regurgitating it. Learning is kinetic and built through careful repetition and practice. Most people know how to type on a computer today because they use it every day. I distinctly remember my dad writing his first book by hand! He was faster at handwriting, and since he never used a computer, he used the most efficient method at hand.

There Is So Much Noise, but Little Action

Increase your people's capacity, and they can handle the increasing demands and also have the flexibility to prioritize and adapt to the fluid demands of today's market. Take a quick look at the fish in the tiny bowl (Figure 3.2). Do you think the fish has much room to maneuver in that small bowl? Imagine if the same fish were living in a 15-gallon aquarium? Imagine if you had a five-gallon bucket to contain 16.9 ounces of daily demand? We don't just need extra capacity for our minds; we need it for our psyches as well. If we don't feel boxed in by our increasing workloads, and if we have 10 times more space to think and innovate, we will feel more capable.

We Are Tool Makers, but Do We Know How to Use the Most Valuable Tool?

Computers are the most remarkable tool we have ever come up with, and it is the equivalent of the bicycle for our minds.

—Steve Jobs

In the 1990 documentary *Memories and Imagination: Pathways to the Library of Congress*, Steve Jobs recounts a study he read about locomotion. In this study, published in *Scientific American*, the goal was to identify which species required the least amount of energy to travel one kilometer. The condor was the most efficient, and humans were hovering around the middle of the pack. Fortunately, someone decided to perform the same test against a human on a bicycle. Even with a crude turn-of-the-century model, a person with a bike was the clear winner of the locomotion trials. Jobs then relates that profound insight to the oncoming digital revolution:

> And that's what a computer is to me. What a computer is to me is it's the most remarkable tool that we've ever come up with, and it's the equivalent of a bicycle for our minds.

Jobs often said that what separates us (humans) from other species is that we are tool builders. We will always seek ways to make things better, faster, and, most of all, easier.

Despite the early triumphs of the Apple II and Macintosh, the information superhighway went into relative overdrive when the iPhone hit shelves in 2007. Only 10 years later, 60 percent of the world accesses the Internet through a mobile device every day. Imagine life without always-on social media, e-mail, and a personal computer just a swipe away. Never before has one person had the ability to consume this much information with next to no physical effort. Needless to say, our brains are fundamentally ill-equipped to handle this daily bombardment—let alone how to act on any of it.

Jobs and other tech pioneers have vastly improved the efficiency and output of the modern world. But what we must remember is that these are ultimately tools—devices or instruments to carry out a particular function. Currently, we are beholden to the tools, in many cases allowing them to control us. Tools were meant to be used by us, not vice versa. There's never been a better time to upgrade our capacity to enable us to use these powerful tools more effectively.

No technology or future technology will ever come close to matching human creativity, adaptability, flexibility or compassion.
—Dr. Phil Nuernberger, author of *Strong and Fearless*

2. Stress Is Melting Us Down

We Are Both the Source and the Solution for Stress

Stress management, mindfulness, meditation, and conscious capitalism are all buzzwords floating around organizations trying to battle the stress monster gobbling up everyone's emotional energy. What is stress exactly? Does your culture show troubling signs of stress? Is stress good or bad? Is it possible to eliminate stress altogether?

Stress

We are starting to understand the physiological impacts and psychological triggers rooted in chronic stress. There is compelling evidence showing that we have more stress today than ever before. More and more people aren't able to regulate the mounting pressure. Our psyches are starting to resemble old worn-out basketballs. They either are about to explode from too much pent-up anxiety or are outright deflated from trying to bear the weight of it.

Your parents or grandparents are probably quick to judge today's generation for not having to work nearly as hard as they did. In some obvious respects, they had it so much harder. They didn't have the ease of instant communication or access to the entire world's information at their fingertips. But despite how much less physically taxing today's environment is, its psychological toll is far greater. We rely on our intellect more than our brawn to earn a place in society more than any previous generation.

So, what does this have to do with stress? The real reason for all this rampant increase in anxiety and stress, along with record levels of depression and mania, is the overwhelming complexity of our interconnected world. It is so severe that according to the American Psychological Association, teens reported higher average stress levels (5.8 on a 10-point scale) than adults (5.1) for the very first time.

Why is this happening? Are there more lions, tigers, and bears to dodge? Is the plague or risk of infection lurking around the corner? No, in fact we are statistically safer than ever before—despite what your local news programming might tell you. What has changed is the overstimulation and processing our brains endure on daily basis. These stressor inputs are called *mind chatter* and determine how we process and perceive immediate threats.

What If We Simplified Stress?

Stress is physiological not psychological. Stress is merely a symptom of a precieved threat, and it differs greatly for each one of us. Some people are fearful of public speaking and can quickly experience enough stress to induce physical nausea or vomiting—a physical symptom. Some of us are incredibly stressed out about possible catastrophes—like an asteroid hitting the planet or a devastating earthquake. But almost all of us can relate to the mounting stress of having way too much on our minds at any given moment. Our weekdays become carefully timed routines that are already stressful enough to maintain and downright debilitating if we ever deviate from them in the slightest.

Now that we've established that stress is physiological, let's let out a collective exhale. There's hope after all, because we can control it! Stress doesn't have to dictate our reactions and how we get through the day. Stress can be managed by building resilience and mindfulness into our day. We can conquer stress by developing thought patterns that recycle potential stressors into motivational fuel.

Stress is too harmful to our minds and bodies to ignore any longer. Building capacity will give you and your people the ability to cope with stress.

In later chapters, we will talk about focus, attention, and rest. If you teach yourself how to get better rest and focus on the right outcomes, your stress will diminish and hopefully curb a dependence on various forms of self-medication (such as alcohol and prescription drugs). Let's arm your people with the ammunition to fend off those lions, tigers, and bears in the modern jungle of complexity.

3. We Over-Rely on Skills and Talent

Most of us have enjoyed playing a spirited game of Jenga. If you haven't yet, each player's goal is to remove one block from a 54-block tower, and place it on top, without the whole structure tumbling down. There is even a delightful life-sized Jenga where the pieces are much larger and the tower quickly reaches a height where you have to use a step stool to reach the top. Regardless of the version, the outcome is always inevitably the same. Just don't be left holding the last block.

Jenga

But imagine if the rules were modified and allowed for players to expand the foundation by adding blocks to the side. Instead of a teetering top-heavy tower of 54 blocks, you could have a large pyramid constructed from 154 blocks that's nearly indestructible.

Recently a news outlet interviewed our company On Target Living about organizational development and asked what kind of companies need capacity training. We couldn't help but chuckle a bit since we get this question fairly often. Most people assume that the people we are talking about or working with are the folks who are considered high performers—the executive team or even the future rising stars. The reality is that everyone needs this training. When trained, everyone in the entire organization will rise up. The tide of increased capacity will raise all ships, and each piece of the puzzle must be notched just right to make the whole enterprise thrive.

In the same interview we talked about working with a sand and gravel association—people responsible for making the aggregate material to build buildings, roads, and structures out of concrete and cement. The very foundation of our country is built with these elemental compounds. One bedrock principle is that you can't build a strong structure without a solid foundation. Construction companies know you can't build a skyscraper without having the best concrete and steel anchoring it at the bottom.

Relying on skill set training and talent alone is like constructing a building from the top down—it's never going to stand the test of time. We hear this more often than you'd think. Let's just go find the best people and everything will solve itself. These companies pay, interview, and assemble esteemed committees to interview and hire the most talented individuals. Once they hire the right people and put them in the right seats, what's the next step?

Over the past 20 years most organizations have created the best departments to find, interview, and hire the best of the best talent. But in this infinitely more complex and demanding landscape, organizations are just hoping the Jenga tower doesn't crumble.

Talent is critical, but you can't go very far with people who don't know the best way to apply it. People who have the greatest capacity for change and application are the ones you want inside an organization. Resiliency is a growing skill that organizations are trying to develop. But if you read the definition of resiliency, it states you must have the capacity to be resilient.

It was once extremely critical for organizations to train their people on skills, and it will continue to be critical in the future, but now that training information is in overwhelming abundance. Much like the written word or a byte of digital storage, its value is based on its scarcity. Leadership, management, and sales consulting firms have 2 million different ways to teach and train. So, are you investing more in these methods because they are important, or because they worked 15 years ago?

Ted St. Martin, a retired dairy farmer, still holds the Guinness World Record for most consecutive free throws made—an astounding 5,221 made in seven hours and 20 minutes.

Do you think Ted is a great basketball player or would be the most valuable player on a team? He would be the first to tell you that he could barely hold his own in a pickup game at your local health club without getting a shot blocked or having the ball stolen every other play. In basketball you must run, jump, dribble, pass, anticipate, and shoot at the right time. If you assembled a basketball team solely based on specialty skills, then you would probably pick world record holders in free throws, high jump, and sprinting. Obviously this team would be a train wreck because they aren't well-rounded basketball players; they're just elite performers of one particular skill. Organizational success isn't based on a smattering of isolated skills. It's based on elevating the level of play for all the interconnected disciplines throughout.

Mastery is certainly important, and we should all strive for it in moderation. But no amount of mastery is going to give your people the dexterity to handle all the ever-changing demands that emerge in today's economy. There were plenty of programmers that mastered any given language before it was rendered obsolete. The best developers can assimilate and adapt their experiences by having a greater capacity for changing with the current and rolling with the punches so they're always ready for what's next.

4. Engagemnet is Lousy

We need to put the passion back into employee engagement.

Passion is the genesis for all creativity and innovation. Lack of passion isn't a result of organizational practices alone. Nearly every time we look around and try to make eye contact with someone in public, they are either looking down at their phone or just staring blankly ahead—going through the motions. Engagement isn't just a metric on an annual survey. You walk into some organizations and you can immediately feel the air teeming with energy and vitality. Others just zap the energy right out of you.

Employee engagement is undeniably anemic, with a meager 33 percent engagement across all industries. This reminds us of the campy cult classic film *Office Space*, in which the main character, Peter Gibbons, hates his soul-sucking job at the software company Initech. During one scene, he meets with two consultants and explains what a typical work week looks like:

> Well I generally come in 15 minutes late; I use the side door so my boss doesn't see me. From there I space out for about an hour. I just stare at my desk and act like I am working. In a given week, I only actually do about 15 minutes of real, actual work.

Office Space is intended to be a satirical portrayal of the typical white-collar desk-jockey lifestyle. Lousy engagement stats tell us that reality has already arrived.

Many people work to maintain a steady paycheck and provide for their families, but with the newest workplace studies we see that the core motivation for people's professional life is fulfilling their purpose. They aren't driven by the satisfaction of seeing their

The Bobs from *Office Space* (1999)

weekly paycheck deposited or the rare pat on the back for finishing a big project they never understood in the first place. They want to know that their tireless hours of work amount to something substantial and impactful.

At this juncture, it's also important to distinguish between the words *fun* and *engagement*. Just because something is fun, doesn't mean you are engaged. Sure, binge-watching your favorite crime show may feel fun, but it's not engaging. Conversely, fun is not an essential part of engagement. Anyone who has learned to play an instrument for the first time knows how endlessly frustrating and nerve-racking it can be just to tune it properly. Playing becomes fun and engaging after years of practice and knowing all the nuances required to play the instrument well. Engagement is a very diverse metric. It's fun, challenging, purposeful, and acute awareness all at the same time.

Engagement is the real first step in creating the successful culture you desire. If you don't engage your people, it is damn near impossible to educate and create meaningful action. Let's start building people because it's not only the best strategy for your organization but also the right way to earn trust and respect. We see it all the time when we review exit interviews for organizations with high turnover. The overwhelming reason people leave an organization is because they felt they weren't being engaged. They didn't feel they were being used to their full potential. They didn't think management cared about them as people. Engagement is the first step in transformation. It's time to build everyone's capacity for passion and start building each other up the right way.

Engagement + Education + Action = Transformation

5. Our Health Is Embarrassing

Let's say it like it is: the health of corporate America is embarrassing. We are living longer than ever before, but the overall quality of our lives has taken a nosedive.

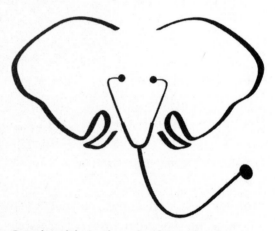

The future of our health is rather bleak if we continue down this unsustainable path (Figure 3.3). We all want to

Our health is the elephant in the room!

live longer lives but maintain a reasonable quality of living. We may not control how long we live, but we can and should do everything we can to preserve our life's quality. Employee health and wellness impact organizations much more than you may imagine. The law of diminishing returns applies not only to adding more people to any production system, but to their health as well. A common example is figuring out the optimal amount of factory line workers for any given part of the industrial process. At a certain point, adding

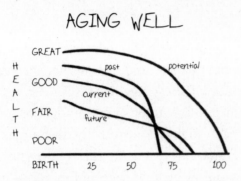

FIGURE 3.3 Aging well.

more people to the line actually diminishes output—way too many cooks in the kitchen. The same rule applies to your people's ability to produce. If they are out sick every other week, or just trying to keep their heads off their desks when they are in for a full week, it's insanity to expect them to handle a full workload.

This isn't a matter of getting to it later. If we don't start taking our people's health seriously and building their capacity to do more, achieving any business objective will be tough sledding indeed.

We were working with a medium-sized insurance company recently. We interviewed the CEO at length about his strategy and tactics for improving his people's health. He said, "My culture isn't really into organic food." He assumed that since his people were unhealthy, they clearly had little to no interest in their own health and well-being. That's when we replied, "Your people will perform better if they feel valued and healthier here. We all spend at least 30 percent of our lives working. Imagine if you and your organization had greater energy, health, and vitality, how would this impact your organization?"

The real challenge and confusion is a lot of business leaders aren't trained to teach their people about living healthier lives. It's not a prerequisite for climbing the corporate ladder. Countless programs tell you what to talk about and what to do, but very few show you *how*.

Medical Illiteracy

Two critical life lessons are not taught in our school systems: how to manage personal finances and how to manage personal health.

We learn about statistics, algebra, essay writing, social studies, and history—but not how to balance a budget or how many hours of sleep to get each night. We probably all remember spending a week in third grade talking about the food pyramid and have a cursory understanding of how digestion works—but not how to actually eat well.

A younger relative of ours reported that calculus is now a required class for all business majors at Michigan State University. After spending a decent amount of time in business, we have never needed to bust out a graphing calculator and figure out the derivative curve of a particular function. The deduction and critical thinking reinforced by calculus is enriching no doubt, but rarely will it be used in application. Your health is your most important asset, and nurturing its growth can only come when we are taught about it.

We mismanage our money and health every single day. Medical illiteracy is simply not an option with the rampant increase of disease and illness across our nation. Doling out more and more copays for needless doctor visits will only increase prescription drugs and diminish quality of life. The more you know, the better questions you can ask, and the more prepared you will be for whatever may come your way.

Many organizations have a biometric screening called "knowing your numbers." But how would an employee improve their numbers if they don't even understand what they are? We aren't recommending you spend hours upon hours researching every disease known to the human race, but you can't be illiterate either.

Do you know what your homocysteine or high sensitive CRP measure? What is your resting heart rate and what does this mean regarding stress management? Did you know that 65% percent of all heart attacks occur with normal cholesterol levels? Did you know that a low testosterone level for both men and women may be due to high levels of stress and lack of rest?

These are the important metrics that most people are heavily confused by or oblivious to.

Hacking versus Methodology

In the sports world, especially golf, the word *hack* is used to describe someone who is not skilled or who lacks the ability to perform at a consistent level. *Hacking* has a slightly more positive connotation in the tech world. Elite hackers are revered for their creative exploits and shortcuts into secure systems and for extracting data without leaving any traces behind. They are twenty-first-century cat burglars exalted for their virtual cunning.

That mentality has seeped into the world of human performance in the form of biohacking—testing your own biology to see what outcomes you can create. This mindset is fueled by our insatiable desire to for instant gratification and quick fixes.

Quick, Easy, Effortless, No Work

It's the same mentality that launched a thousand late-night infomercials. Lose weight without exercising? Doesn't that sound too good to be true? Enough people will buy because it reinforces what they want to hear. But it will fail like the other 46,750 zero-effort weight-loss schemes before it. Your people need a plan to master their own health and wellness—not a get-thin-fast bill of goods. The key to optimal and sustainable performance is practice—not hacking.

If you teach a man to fish, he'll never go hungry again. Let's teach our people how to value and maintain their health so they feel fulfilled and optimized. Hacking your way to the answer and skipping all the lessons along the way is not how we learn. We're wired for overcoming challenges and obstacles on the road to enlightenment. This is the only way we attain wisdom.

Health-Care Costs

We spend 18 percent of our GDP on health care—roughly $3.2 trillion. That's more than the entire GDP of 22 countries! It's almost insulting to call it health care, because our health outcomes are not getting any better despite an expected 5 percent annual increase for the foreseeable future.

Here is a list of the top 15 lifestyle-related conditions for which Americans take medications that suck productivity and cost organizations the most money. Seventy percent of Americans take at least one prescription medication to treat the following and more than 50 percent take two:

1. High cholesterol
2. Hypothyroidism
3. Hypertension
4. Acid reflux/GERD
5. Type 2 diabetes
6. Pain/Inflammation
7. ADHD
8. Fibromyalgia
9. Psoriasis
10. Arthritis
11. Depression
12. Asthma
13. Sleep
14. Bone health
15. Digestive health

Almost all these conditions are lifestyle related. Medications taken for these issues merely treat the symptoms of chronic poor health.

Two of the newest and fastest-growing medications are fueled by the chronic stress epidemic sweeping across the corporate landscape:

- Antidepressants (10–12 percent of the population; 25 percent for women in their 40s and 50s)
- Medications to treat attention deficit/hyperactivity disorder (adults receiving prescriptions for ADHD has doubled in the past several years, not to mention the adults using it without a script.)

It is estimated that the amount of ADHD medication sold in 2020 will total $17.5 billion. To put that number in perspective, coffee (America's favorite stimulant) brings in $30 billion annually.

This is the 10-ton elephant in the room, suffocating your profitability and performance. Employers invest billions of dollars in health and wellness solutions, creating benefit programs that try to manage risk and provide value to the employees, yet health and performance outcomes have not improved at a commensurate rate. We have better access to premier hospital systems, highly trained health professionals, and cutting-edge medical technology. So why do we keep falling down the list of world's healthiest countries?

What if the problem isn't health-care policy, the environment, or incentives in the workplace? What if the real problem is our mindset on health and performance in the workplace? What if our mindset on health and performance was similar to the mindset on leadership, management, marketing, and sales?

We cannot fix the health-care problem by simply making our health-care system more affordable and efficient. Imagine if everyone looked at health care from a new perspective? Having more healthy people should be our goal, not more health-care options!

All companies want a healthier workforce, but the strategy is siloed off to the HR staff or voluntary committee. It's rarely even mentioned in the initial onboarding process let alone a key component of ongoing training and development. How can we expect better health to underscore better performance when it's not integrated from day one!

We worked with a company that has an amazing learning and development platform. It's the centralized platform to grow and evolve their workforce and is focused on customer service, team-work, time management, and leadership.

They also have an initiative to cut health-care costs since it is the second highest expense next to wages. But this excellent initia-tive was completely separated from their award-winning learning and development platform. It's almost like storing your silverware and napkins in the kitchen, but stashing the plates and cups down in the basement—it doesn't make for an enjoyable dining experi-ence. This strategy hamstrings any organization because it doesn't tie health to performance in a concrete way. You need to connect the dots and show people how better *focus*, *energy*, and *drive* create endless opportunities for growth and prosperity.

Today the best organizations understand the importance of col-laboration. The marketing team needs to meet with research and development to start thinking about how to position upcoming products in the marketplace. Accounting needs to collaborate with facilities managers to anticipate any upcoming capital projects. Your training and development should be built on the foundation of peak performance. You want your associates, executives, and sales teams to be all they can be. But they can't maximize their potential if you don't teach them how to manage their stress and wake up energized and alert.

We know an organization is simply people with a purpose. The five major obstacles presented in this chapter prevent people and organizations from achieving and exceeding that purpose. What drives us is the desire to teach people how to be their best selves so they can do great things together. An organization is only as strong and successful as the health of its people. It builds their capacity for optimal performance and overachievement.

Now that we've set the table for *building capacity*, it's time to start serving up the recipe for better health and performance through enhanced *focus*, *energy*, and *drive*.

Key Point

Five Problems
1. Demands are increasing and capacity is shrinking.
2. Stress is melting us down.
3. We overrely on skills and talent.
4. Engagement is lousy.
5. Our health is embarrassing.

4 Human Capital Is the Future!

Keeneland, Kentucky, is one of the top venues for thoroughbred horseracing. The Saturdays in the fall remind you of a college football atmosphere—the energy is electric! Everyone is decked out—the men in their suits and ties, and the women in their dresses and hats. One by one the horses for each race come out. If you have never seen a thoroughbred racehorse up close, this is a sight to see. These animals are perfect. They are graceful, sleek, and muscular; their eyes are clear and their coats are shiny and colorful. They are built for speed! Every horse looks extremely fit and fast, but only some have what it takes to be the best.

Winning the United States Triple Crown is the pinnacle of thoroughbred horseracing. Since 1875, the first year in which all three races occurred, only 12 horses have accomplished this rare feat.

What makes winning the Triple Crown so elusive? Capacity! The winner must have a combination of speed, strength, endurance, intelligence, and lots of grit. It is very difficult to measure grit or heart—but every Triple Crown winner must have the heart to push beyond his or her comfort zone!

The Triple Crown consists of three races:

- Kentucky Derby—1¼ miles
- Preakness Stakes—1³⁄₁₆ miles
- Belmont Stakes—1½ miles

The Kentucky Derby is a sprint, at just over a mile. The Belmont Stakes is the longest of the three races and is a beast, a real test of endurance and heart. To win the Triple Crown, the entire racing team—including the trainer, jockey, and horse—must have the capacity to perform in all three distances under varying conditions.

Now imagine if you owned a $5 million thoroughbred racehorse. How would you take care of your racehorse? Most likely you would do everything in your power to protect your investment; you would give your horse all the resources it needed to perform at its best: plenty of rest, quality water, only the most nutritious grasses and grains, and the right amount of exercise.

Now compare a thoroughbred racehorse to a typical mule working on a farm. In most cases the mule is overworked and undernourished; the owner is trying to get the most out of the mule before it begins to break down! We see this happening more and more within many organizations. Even though it is not the intent, organizations aren't treating their people in a way that creates peak performance. As demands continue to grow, how is your organization investing in its future? How is it investing in its people?

Growing Your Greatest Resource

As the organizational landscape continues to change, the way we currently develop our people is growing obsolete. What does the future of your organization hold? What does the future of your organization need? When it comes to the future of creating the best organizations or making the greatest impact on our world, the obvious sign is our people—people are the future.

Human capital is our greatest resource and in many cases also our most overlooked resource. We are looking externally versus internally to find methods to increase performance and increase profitability. We have become fixated on the power of technology, but we have become ignorant of the infinite ability of the human mind and body!

Technology advances have been incredible and will continue to expand and grow: computers, smartphones, electronic devices, social media platforms, satellites, space travel, virtual reality, military, IT developments—the list is long and will continue to make a huge impact on our world. What if we invested at a similar pace in our people? The long-term differentiator of any organization when compared to others is *people*, the mind and body behind the technology.

In 2017 the United States launched the most expensive military ship in history, the USS *Gerald R. Ford* (Figure 4.1), which came in at over $10 billion—$12.8 billion to be exact. The USS *Gerald R. Ford* is an incredible military advancement and an incredible capital investment; there is no denying the power and performance capabilities. One fact many forget is that it is complemented by 5,000 people. Imagine if the mindset around expanding human capital was equally as important, if not more?

What if we became as sophisticated at using our human resources as we are with our technology resources?

The History Channel had a series called *The Selection: Special Operations Experiment*, produced by Peter Berg. This show places 30 men and women with no military background through the most intense physical and mental challenge of their lives. These 30 individuals are led by veterans of the Navy SEALs, Green Berets, and Army Rangers. The instructors try to push the 30 individuals as far as they can go. Only 4 of the 30 make it. During episode 3,

FIGURE 4.1   Military ship.

Bert Kuntz, a veteran Green Beret, had a wonderful description of the value of human capital and what it means for the future:

> The United States military has hands down the most expensive military equipment in the history of the world, but hands down the most precious equipment it has and will always have is humans.

As with the USS *Gerald R. Ford* and other advances and innovations, let's look toward the future, but let's start by building the foundation of our greatest resource.

Foundational Pillars

If you were going to build any organization from the ground up, what would you do? Where would you begin? I think most would agree, to build the best organization you would begin with people—go out and get the best and brightest people. If this is true, then what?

Many of us have studied or heard of Abraham Maslow's hierarchy of human needs (Figure 4.2) and how it relates to the needs and desires of people. Maslow, an American psychologist, noticed while working with monkeys that certain needs take precedence

FIGURE 4.2 Maslow's hierarchy of needs.

over others. Maslow discovered that the monkeys would not move up their hierarchy of needs until the needs below were met. For example, if the monkeys were thirsty, drinking would take precedence over eating and up the hierarchy they would go. Maslow created his hierarchy of human needs based on what he learned from his studies with monkeys. Maslow then laid out his five layers of human needs: physiological needs, safety, love and belonging, esteem, and self-actualization.

The first four levels of needs Maslow calls *deficit needs*—if you don't have enough of something, you have a deficit, so you feel the need. The last level of Maslow's hierarchy of human needs is self-actualization. Maslow referred to this level as growth motivation. These needs do not involve balance. As they get stronger, the more attention we give them. They involve the continuous desire to fulfill potentials. If you truly want to self-actualize, then you must have your lower needs met first.

You might be thinking, "What does Maslow's hierarchy of human needs have to do with greater success for me and my organization?" Maslow believed that every person has a strong desire to realize their full potential, to reach a level of self-actualization—finding the positive potential of human beings. Maslow's theory is that people enjoy peak experiences, high points in life, when they are in harmony with themselves and their surroundings. Maslow believed self-actualized people could have many peak experiences throughout the day, whereas others who do not have this foundation have very few high points. We are fascinated when we listen to people express their needs: working on their career, making more money, buying a new house or new car, developing personal relationships, finding their purpose, and most importantly, improving their health.

We find it interesting that in our society, some of our most basic physiological human needs are so often neglected. For many, taking care of the fundamental needs is not even on their radar screen.

It becomes difficult to perform at your best when you don't get enough sleep, eat poorly, and rarely move your body. Taking the escalator to the top is not how you get to your fullest potential.

Beginning or End

One of the barriers we face while consulting with organizations is that companies don't see the need for health within their organization. For many organizations, health and wellness are extremely low on the priority list—things to put on the *nice to have* list, but not truly necessary as a strategy within the organization. Many organizations have a wellness program currently in place, but many do not have a clear plan or vision of what outcomes or metrics they would like to change, and the program isn't integrated in training and development.

A few years ago, we were asked to do a keynote presentation for a large health-care provider. We were extremely excited to have the opportunity to showcase how we could help improve the health and performance throughout the entire organization. The feedback and evaluations were great, the engagement was fantastic, and people loved our message. We asked, "What is your strategy for the future?" We were then steered to their wellness team. We set up a meeting with their wellness team and quickly discovered that they did not have a wellness team—this large health-care organization of over 8,000 people had a wellness team of one. This one person was extremely passionate in helping improve the health and performance of the organization but was not given the resources to make this happen. She was overwhelmed and extremely frustrated that senior leadership was not on board.

Times Are Changing!

We believe the most successful organizations are beginning to recognize they have to play a larger role in the overall health of their people. They have to get in the game and take more responsibility and become the positive influence that many people so desperately need.

People spend 80,000–100,000 hours of their life at work. Add to this number the hours devoted to commuting, and our work is the largest investment of our time. For many people work can also be the most stressful factor in their life; in fact, 43 percent of people consider work to be their number-one stressor. Stress affects everything from our energy, our ability to focus, how much drive we have, how we sleep, how we eat, how we move, and our overall health and performance!

What if your organization was the number-one source of positive influence? What if your organization actively and intentionally was the number-one source for greater well-being, satisfaction, and happiness? What if people were happier and healthier because of work? Imagine creating an organizational culture that was driving this mindset, this entirely new way of thinking?

Creating Wealth

Consider the difference between working with an insurance agent and with a financial adviser. Almost everyone and every organization has insurance, but not everyone has a financial adviser. Insurance is mostly a commodity-driven business; people are looking for the greatest coverage at the lowest rate. Insurance is to protect you; it's the security blanket, and it's the peace of mind that if something unfortunate happened, you would be covered. Many organizations provide insurance and other benefits for their employees—smoking-cessation classes, weight-loss programs, Fitbits, blood pressure screenings, lunch and learns—all trying to protect their investment, their people. Having these types of commodity programs and initiatives in place is nice but will not create transformation and increased performance. Having a financial adviser, on the other hand, is all about managing and growing your wealth. The financial advisers begin by protecting your current wealth, but the real goal of the financial advisor is to grow your wealth, not just protect it. Imagine if your organization took the financial-advisory approach, first by protecting and then by investing in their people to help them grow.

Performance Outcomes

The thought of investing in human capital isn't new; it actually isn't even a radical shift in thinking for most organizations. The shift comes in the form of *how to* get there and *how to* invest. Most people want to know what outcomes they can expect from new actions. To begin your new shift, let's discuss the outcomes that you can expect and the outcomes that are required to win in the future. We call these performance outcomes; to perform at your best, these must be activated.

First, you must be focused on the direction you want to go and have the ability to block out every distraction thrown your way. It's not a matter of just going with the flow; it will come down to knowing exactly what direction you are going. Focus directs your performance.

Second is energy. When you think about fulfilling your purpose, you know the need for energy. The fuel to the engine, the ability to do what it takes—this is energy, and we all know when we have it and when we don't. We will not be able to get by in the future by manufacturing energy. Like the automobile, the desire to burn clean renewable energy is something that will happen. Regarding humans, we will not be able to make energy up if we squander it away. Energy fuels our mission.

Last is the pillar that propels you to the finish line or along the journey. Life is hard and business is harder. If you do not have the

FIGURE 4.3 Performance outcomes.

drive to propel through the muck, you will get stuck and possibly give up. We have all studied the best of the best; every single one had a burning drive that pushed them to their success. When we think of our best selves and our best employees, we are always looking for internal drive—doing the right thing when others aren't looking.

These three performance outcomes (Figure 4.3) are the most critical driving forces to getting the results you desire and fulfilling your mission or purpose. Think about it—is it possible to make the impact you so desire without having *focus*, *energy*, and *drive*?

Capacity Foundation

If the preceding are the three performance outcomes and we have discussed building the foundation first, what are the foundations we must build to expand our capacity? We believe the three foundational pillars that are the bedrock to optimal performance are *REST*, *EAT*, and *MOVE* (Figure 4.4). These are the pillars that most of us control every single day and most organizations have responsibility over. These are not optional, but requirements to have the best performing people possible.

FIGURE 4.4 Pillars for optimal performance.

After more than 30 years, we developed a methodology, with each step building on the next—a straightforward process for increasing performance. No bright lights, no shiny new technology, no energy drinks, no new incentives, no quick fixes, nothing fancy—just straightforward blocking and tackling. This is where the foundation is built and where we believe organizations should begin building capacity.

> **Rest and rejuvenation**—the ability to stop and pause, to recharge, relax, refresh and renew, allowing the body to be young again.
>
> **Eating and nutrition**—the process of being nourished; using food for fuel, growth, and repair.
>
> **Movement and exercise**—the act of physical motion! The human body is designed to move. If movement came in a bottle it would be the most prescribed medication in the world.

In the following six chapters, you will learn *how to* have more *focus*, *energy*, and *drive* by building your bedrock of *REST*, *EAT*, and *MOVE*.

Positive Influence

We have set the table for the rest of the book; in many respects the most valuable portion of the book lies ahead. The blueprints and tactics to the desires and outcomes you are striving for, but before we leave this thought of the future, let's paint an elegant picture of what is possible and what every organization should be thinking.

Currently the workplace is the number-one source of dysfunction in people's lives. Consider this: 43 percent of the population lists work as the most stressful factor in their lives. In earlier chapters we talked about shrinking capacity, demands, stress, overload, health issues, and many other dysfunctions. People spend 90,000 hours of their life at work. Along with that, the average American spends over 10,000 hours commuting.

In Japan, there's a name for overworking: *karoshi*. About 10,000 workers per year drop dead at their desks because of their 70-plus-hour workweeks (not kidding; this really happens).

With married couples, if one person works 10-plus hours a day, it's basically the kiss of death; chances of divorce double. Considering how workplace stress affects everything from sleep to weight gain to ability to focus to overall health and immune function, it's not an overstatement to say most people's work is number-one source of disruption and dysfunction.

But we know we must work, and we know the tremendous opportunities work does give us. So, what if we hit the enhance button for everyone and everything? Consider a future where the workplace is the number-one source of positive influence in an employee's life. What if people were happier and healthier because of work, not in spite of work? This is not a pipe dream. There is a titanic shift happening inside select organizations that are recognizing the need to heavily invest in their human capital.

We are not talking about another wellness plan or a new Fitbit program or an app that provides daily health advice. What if there was an entirely new way to think about the employer-employee relationship. Executive leadership needs to shift into growing and investing in the foundations of human performance.

You want to dramatically improve engagement and reap all the sweet rewards associated with high-performing teams? Treat your people as you would your wealth. Take a long-term view and own the responsibility for influencing them in a positive way.

You have influence right now.

You have the power right now.

How are you using it?

If you see the need and see a solution, then it's your responsibility to do something.

The future workplace that is going to win business initiatives and people initiatives is going to create influence.

Everybody fears change: the fear of failure and the anxiety about too much work and too much to do. The biggest fear we see is lack of change, because as we have noted, the world is speeding up, and if we don't get in front of it we will lag behind.

Key Point

Human capital is the foundation to the future and it always will be. You can't run a ship without the people!

5 Laser *Focus* Directs Performance

People think focus means saying yes to the thing you've got to focus on. But that's not what it means at all. It means saying NO to the hundred other good ideas that there are. You have to pick carefully.
—Steve Jobs

What skills do you think top organizations consider most critical to fuel future growth?

We surveyed hundreds of clients across many different industries, dedicating considerable resources toward the following core competencies:

1. Creativity and innovation
2. Leadership
3. Customer service
4. Resiliency
5. Time management
6. Teamwork and communication
7. Organization
8. Sales

These buzzwords would surround anyone walking down the business section of their local bookstore. Business and thought leaders alike can't seem to churn out enough TED Talks that riff on one of these hot topics. Most executives we consult with expect every new hire and leaders to embody all eight of these behaviors and traits. All of these skills are arguably the most desirable qualities of any working professional. So, what we really should be asking ourselves is what they all have in common. What fuels creativity and innovation? What builds resiliency? How do you manage your time effectively?

In reality, the most important skill is *focus/attention*.

Cal Newport, author of *Deep Work*, argues that focus is the new IQ and is essential to thriving in the knowledge economy:

> To remain valuable in our economy, therefore, you must master the art of quickly learning complicated things. This task requires deep work. If you don't cultivate this ability, you're likely to fall behind as technology advances.

Cal makes a compelling argument that many of us have shifted from deep work to shallow work. We are all fighting this uphill battle in the effort for productivity gains. The average attention span has dropped from 12 seconds in 2000 to 8 seconds in 2013 and is still diminishing rapidly. Imagine a race car driver texting during the race or a surgeon checking his e-mail in the operating room.

Now amplify this to the nanosecond speed of information. The average mobile user taps, swipes, and clicks their phone 2,617 times each day, and heavy users engage with their smartphones 5,427 times. How can we expect to keep up if we are constantly distracted?

Media saturation has inflated the value of attention to an all-time high. The baseline KPI for any advertising campaign is CPM, or cost per thousand impressions. An impression is your attention, even if it's less than a second. Social media platforms now have billion-dollar valuations (with no actual profit) because they dominate your attention. In many ways, these always-on social networks have removed nearly all communication boundaries that previously existed between us. A text message requires drastically less investment than a phone call. A snap requires even less investment than a text message. These networks don't care about the content of your message. Like all information systems, they want to transmit more data with less energy.

From a physiological standpoint, too much of this type of hyper-connectivity can be dangerously addictive and draining. Dopamine is our body's reward chemical and is released by our brain each time we receive positive feedback. Runner's high, a pat on the back after a great presentation, or a simple hug all trigger different levels of dopamine rushes we all crave. Social media is a dopamine delivery system on steroids. Each like, comment, or friend request is based on the expectation of acceptance from those around you. Unlike a hug or verbal expression, though, these shallow signals are poor forms of social feedback. How many times have you liked something on Facebook because of the image alone? Did you read the actual post itself or the comments? How much time do we really spend deciding how to engage with the tens of thousands of posts we consume each month?

Just like any other addiction, the habit becomes ingrained to an irrational level. Have you ever felt your phone vibrate and reached into your pocket, only to discover that it never vibrated at all? Phantom vibration syndrome is just one alarming symptom of our overdependence on digital media and our inability to unplug from it. It's ultimately the catch-22 of this new century. How do you stay connected without losing your focus? How do you manage these tools while building your most critical skill?

The $50 Million Opportunity

No timeline is shorter for greatness than that of a professional athlete. There's very little margin for error and the clock never stops ticking on the relentless pursuit of perfection. Our work with athletes is a great example of the opportunity and challenges we all have. When we work with someone one-on-one, athlete or not, we start with a discovery session. This open-ended interview helps customize a plan to meet and hopefully exceed the person's desired outcomes. We ask what they want and look for ways to unlock their *why*. This allows us to build small action steps together to achieve their goals.

In the case of athletes, they are very passionate about what they should eat, how to exercise, and ways to recover faster. They want to fire on all cylinders. They crave peak performance and don't want to waste any time getting there. Their *why* is usually anchored in self-actualization and seeing how good they can be. However, they tend to overlook the one critical factor that enables elite performance. It's a skill that few practice but could untimely land them a $10 million, $20 million, or $50 million contract: *focus*. For many athletes, it's that elusive missing element to the success they worked so hard to achieve.

Two common focus problems:
  1. No plan
  2. No skill

No plan: Imagine a super-talented hockey player. He has been drafted at a young age based on raw talents and abilities. The organization that drafted him is convinced he can develop into an integral part of the team. Here's the problem: they don't have a clear plan or process to maximize his potential; they just go with the flow and let the chips fall where they may. There is no manual for blocking out distractions. There's no guide for managing a grueling practice schedule and family life. The player hasn't been taught how to say no and focus his energy toward constant self-improvement—on and off the ice. He is always trying new things without following a clearly defined course. It's hard to master your craft when you feel aimless and unable to set a course toward success.

No skill: This is our favorite situation. A basketball player has all the skills and talent on the court. She can even perform under pressure and hit the clutch shot, but can't seem to dial in on a consistent basis. Some stuff is important and other stuff isn't, but there doesn't seem to be any rhyme or reason to it. The player knows she lacks focus, but has never been shown how to focus. She simply lacks the tools to unlock her full potential. She hasn't learned how to focus yet.

These two examples are what we see every day. If aspiring players could channel their focus, what is possible—a $50 million contract?

Nick Saban is arguably the greatest college football coach of all time. He's created a seemingly unstoppable dynasty at the University of Alabama. Ask any of his players and coaches the secret to his stunning success, and they will all tell you the same thing: *he is laser focused and lives in the present.* You can ultimately only control your effort and execution. Let go of the past results and don't let the future rule you either. Embrace the moment, forget about what you can't control, and focus on the next shot or next play. Don't let your entourage or the media determine your future. Control the narrative on the field of play, and let the chips fall where they may.

Obviously, many of you reading this will not be signing eight-figure contracts. You probably don't have as much downtime or distractions either, but the challenges are the same. Your organization may have a lot more to lose if you don't prioritize focus. It may be finishing that big project or closing a deal with a major client. In the digital world we live in, focus is the ultimate differentiator.

Mind over Matter

It's not the chatter of people around us that is the most powerful distractor, but rather the chatter of our own minds.
—Daniel Goleman, author of *Focus: The Hidden Power of Excellence*

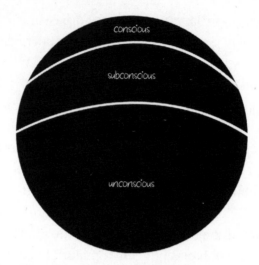

FIGURE 5.1 The three levels of the mind.

Arguably the most important sign of life is how something responds to stimuli. How do you process everything happening around you without being completely distracted? It all starts with your mind and how it processes the world around you. Your mind has three stages of consciousness that filter your perception and thought. To learn how to focus, you need to understand the basics of the mind. (See Figure 5.1.)

Stage 1: Self-Awareness↔Conscious Mind

The first step in changing behavior, or even knowing the right action to take, is self-awareness. It's the ability to step outside yourself for a moment in order to make a calculated or conscious decision. Unlike subconscious thought, this is a completely internal reaction to the world around us. It's a more proactive action instead of a subconscious reaction to everything swirling around us. This ideal level of consciousness is what separates humans from the rest of the animal kingdom. We have the ability to weigh all possible reactions to our actions before we take them. But time is in increasingly short supply, and conscious thinking doesn't always provide the path of least resistance to get the job done. For many of us, on a daily basis, conscious thinking is suboptimal for the following reasons:

- Slower processing
- Amount of effort required
- Limited information

In order to achieve sustainable focus and clarity, we must also be self-aware. Many managers sometimes make decisions based largely on what their direct competitors are doing. This makes sense on the surface. If the rest of the market is clearly moving in one direction, shouldn't we be devoting more resources to pivot in that direction as well? A new strategy is one thing, but executing it is an entirely different animal and requires buy-in at every level. So, before you go all-in on a new product offering or marketing campaign, make sure you step back and reflect on this important question—do I really believe in this? If you do, then changing your team's dynamic and processes won't be nearly as difficult because you can instill that belief in your team and more easily empower them to focus on a singular goal. The conscious mind can form or reform the subconscious mind.

Stage 2: Autopilot↔Subconscious Mind

The best way to respond to an overstimulated situation is to switch on mental autopilot—the subconscious mind. This second level of consciousness allows us to process information much faster with considerably less energy. If work starts to become more repetitive and tedious, which it has with more and more people using digital tools for everyday tasks, then our brains have to find the path of least resistance to get the job done quickly. This is the level where your habits live and why it is important to build good habits. Here are a few more reasons why subconscious engagement has become the new normal for many workplaces and their people:

- Speed
- Energy conservation
- Task switching "multitasking"
- Habits
- Amount of information to process
- Demands
- Time
- Memory

Before computers ever existed, we had to rely on our brains alone to handle the repetitive tasks of previous generations. Picking crops, threshing wheat, or churning butter were all necessary routine tasks that needed to be performed every day. The critical difference now is that the mindless chores of today require very little manual labor. Our brain is still wired to expect all of the senses to be triggered during this stage of consciousness, but in many cases, our primary sensory input is simply staring at a screen and typing on a keyboard. The work itself is still mentally taxing, but it is less rewarding since we aren't receiving any of the benefits of physical labor (dopamine/endorphin rush, increased heart rate, etc.). You may feel productive checking all of these tasks off your daily to-do list, but this auto-pilot leaves very little time to focus on building and creating new things.

Stage 3: Endless Galaxy↔Unconscious

Do you know that there are at least 100 billion galaxies in the known universe? Trying to wrap your head around that is impossible because it's infinite—it literally cannot be quantified. This is similar to the unconscious mind—the limitless reservoir of knowledge, creativity, and experiences that makes up the other 85 percent of our brain we can't directly access, yet still has tremendous influence over our behavior and decision making. Do you ever catch yourself daydreaming? Thinking about an experience or idea or thought that came out of the blue? Whether it's staring out a window aimlessly at work or fixing your gaze on a favorite painting at home, our minds always have a tendency to wander when they are idle. It's hard not to feel a little guilty once you snap back to reality—"I can't afford to waste time daydreaming today!" But recent research proves quite the opposite—daydreaming and idle thought may be the most valuable use of your time.

- Critical thinking—Unconscious thinking effortlessly builds connections between the *conscious* (self-awareness) and *subconscious* (autopilot) parts of the brain.
- Enhanced insight—Professors Benjamin Baird and Jonathan Schooler have proven that taking a few moments to daydream and reflect on a new task leads to more insightful responses than immediately focusing on the solution. Have you ever been in the shower or in the middle of sleep and you came up with a great idea? This is the true power of the mind; it usually has the answer if you allow it to go there.
- Problem solving—"Your mind-wandering capacity is like that computer program—it can get to solutions that your conscious mind just can't see."—Amy Fries, *Daydreams at Work: Wake Up Your Creative Powers*
- Improved concentration—Even a 30-second break from a difficult task can increase your focus.
- Better productivity—The Pomodoro Technique breaks up work into 25-minute sessions with short five-minute breaks between them. After four sessions, the breaks become 15 minutes and give your brain more time to reflect and form new neural connections.

The unconscious mind holds the answers to many questions and problems. Because of its infinite capacity, the unconscious can be the most powerful part of the brain. To access this information on demand takes training and the ability to quiet the mind; it takes deliberate practice.

Our focus level depends on which consciousness we tap into at any given moment. We need all three to function, but you aren't reading this book just to scrape by on irrational fear-based reactions. You want to attain a higher level of focus that comes from an active rhythm of conscious and unconscious thought. That's the bedrock to building a foundation of sustained clarity of vision despite all the distractions. Now let's take a closer look at how to avoid distraction through better attention.

Attention Spectrum

Engagement

The science behind focus is actually fairly straightforward. There are two ends to the focus spectrum, and the ultimate goal is to favor the engagement and interest end. When we are engaged and internally interested in something, we can focus on it for hours on end without our performance diminishing. Think about something in your life in which you were fully engaged. Maybe it was writing, solving a complicated math problem, painting, playing music, or spending quality time with the kids. Now think of all the stuff you aren't engaged in—probably taxes, mandatory meetings, driving in traffic, or waiting in the grocery checkout line, just to list a few. What do you notice about your focus? How does your performance differ?

A key distinction worth stressing is that engagement and interest do not always mean entertainment, enjoyment, and pleasure. In this age of instant gratification, we sometimes forget to find interest and engagement in the little things or the stuff that challenges us. This could be a big part of tackling focus and attention for you and your organization. Next time you say or hear your team say that something was boring or not interesting, ask yourself or them, "Is this something important and could it make you better?" If so, find the smallest detail to gain your interest or engagement. This practice will allow you to develop the ability to engage on demand and focus when needed. It's muscle memory for paying attention, and we end up wanting to learn more. Some of the best outcomes come from things we didn't want to do; these small incremental actions lead to better results down the road. The lack of engagement is truly the root cause of the lack of focus. Find engagement and you will find focus.

Fear

The other end of the attention spectrum is fear. As we alluded to earlier, fear can fuel a false sense of focus. Fear creates a mere tunnel vision of focus with very limited ability or awareness to adapt to change. Ever cringe at that e-mail where you didn't get the business, beat yourself up for making a huge mistake like double booking an important meeting, or feel ashamed after forgetting a loved one's birthday? You get sick to your stomach, and all you can think about is what you did wrong. You become completely detached from the present and start fixating on the past or future—which you can't control.

I (Matt) remember an e-mail that I received one Friday afternoon on my way to my annual buddy golf trip. It was from a prospective client that I was confident we were going land. We went through all the steps: We did eight months of follow-up and follow-through, brought out all the bells and whistles, and jumped through all kinds of hoops to deliver what I thought they wanted. Much to my chagrin, they politely explained why we didn't earn the business and why they didn't see the long-term value in our services. On this sunny and beautiful summer Michigan day, I made the mistake of allowing fear to dictate my focus. I immediately started to dwell on my failure and question the viability of our business model if we couldn't close this deal. This wasn't the first rejection we'd received, nor would it be the last, but for whatever reason it shook me to my core. I couldn't stop thinking about this e-mail and let it cloud my judgment and mood despite the trip's potential enjoyment.

After the dust settled, it became clear just how much I blew this one shortcoming out of proportion. It was a humbling reminder that we can't always get what we want. Now when I receive these types of letdowns, I have a strategy and plan to not allow fear to dictate my thoughts and subsequent actions. I instead focus on the improvements needed and engage on what I can control. When you think about it, fear is largely fueled by future visions that have yet to happen. Today's workforce and leadership have more fear than ever before. It's not a question of avoiding fear; it's an answer of how you are going to perceive this threat with your mind. Most fear is not in the present moment. It's in the past or future. This ultimately means it's not real!

Boredom

In the middle of the spectrum and what takes up the most space in our lives is boredom. Don't think of boredom as a bad thing. Whether it's another mind-sucking meeting or a conversation with your lovely neighbor about her five cats, it's an inevitable fact of life. Our brains operate in a bored state longer than you may think—about half of the day according to recent studies. This mindless time allows us to preserve energy while still creating thousands of new neural pathways that fuel creativity and concentration. We will talk about energy in the next chapter and how to improve and sustain it, but in the context of focus, boredom is simply the lack of attention (Figure 5.2).

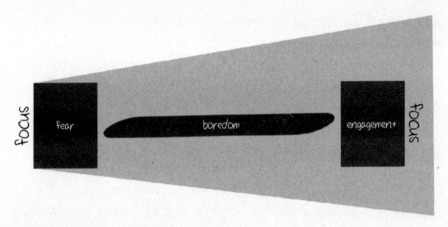

FIGURE 5.2 Focus spectrum.

Boredom is also important because it's the exact opposite of engagement. Like any of our other emotions, it's felt most sharply when the affirmative or positive side of the spectrum is absent. If we are living in constant fear of failure or cruising along on autopilot through a sea of boredom long enough, we stop seeking real engagement. We've trained ourselves to operate at a lower level than our infinite capacity. We must spend more time paying attention and engaging with the stuff that actually matters.

How to Focus

If your primary reason for reading this book is to optimize yourself and your organization, then your first goal should be paying attention. What if everyone had the ability to completely concentrate on the things they were destined to do?

Three Tactics to Increase Focus
1. Breathing
2. Cancel the noise
3. Practice

In the *REST*, *EAT*, *MOVE* chapters we will talk about other things that improve your focus, like getting enough sleep, whitespace, superfoods, meditation, and daily movement. For this chapter, start building the following specific tactics into your everyday routines. This is your focus toolbox; follow them in this order.

Breathing

One of the most powerful and effective methods to focus is learning how to use breath awareness and belly breathing to quiet the mind. We will take a deeper dive into this in Chapter 8, "REST," but it is necessary to understand when talking about focus tactics. Belly breathing and breath awareness is the *only* way we can internally quiet the mind. The human body basically has two ways to breathe—*chest breathing*, or survival breathing, and *belly breathing*, or optimal breathing. Try this exercise to start practicing belly breathing:

First, if possible lay on your back in a comfortable position. If you can't lie down, sit upright in a chair with your chest up and shoulders back. Inhale through your nose; feel the slight coolness of your breath and bring all of your attention there. Next, exhale through your nose, feeling the air passing back out through your nose; bring your attention there. Do this for 10–15 seconds and keep your attention on the act of breathing alone. Try not to let your mind wander and simply be in the moment.

Pause—what are you thinking about? Is it possible to focus on your breath and your thoughts at the same time? Of course not! It's a powerful yet simple truth. Our minds can only focus on one thing at a time.

Once you have your breath awareness down, aim your attention at your belly. As you inhale your belly should rise. The belly will fall smoothly once you exhale. You should have no movement in your chest. This is the first exercise to train the diaphragm—which happens to be the second most important muscle in the human body (first is the heart). When we start to practice our breathing, we can begin to learn how to quiet the mind and create true focus.

This is an exercise we recommend doing daily, hourly, or when you need to focus, reduce stress, and execute. Breathing is our most powerful tool to manage the mind. Most of us neglect that power because breathing is an autonomic act. Now that you know the key to optimal breathing, you can quiet the mind during any stressful moment and make a conscious decision on your next move or action.

Cancel the Noise

Do you own a pair of noise-cancelling headphones? Over the past five-plus years it seems the growth of the headphone business has exploded. Everywhere you look, people are wearing these large almost goofy-looking noise-cancelling headphones. Companies like Bose and Beats are leading the way.

Now we understand this concept of canceling the outside noise to enjoy your entertainment, but how do we apply it to our daily lives? What will this noise cancellation do for our focus and performance? This tactic is one that we find people know about, even dream about, but don't know how to execute. How do you know what is noise and what isn't? Does this mean you should be rude and unapproachable? Can you imagine life with two or three more hours of quality time a day to work on what you are meant to do? How much time in your day is unnecessary noise?

Here is how you cancel noise:

Step 1: *What outcome do you want?* To truly block out noise, you must know where you are going. Start with this simple question—what outcome do you want? If you achieved this outcome would you consider it a huge success? Think big. What is possible? What are you capable of?

Step 2: Create a plan or process. After you have set the outcome you desire—whether it's bringing in $11 million of new business in Q3 or finishing the concept for the next product—it's time to work backward. What is the timeline? Who needs to be involved? What actions need to be taken every month, week, and day? Build a clear process that outlines a roadmap to the very likely achievement of your goals. That's the critical point: you can't control the outcome; you only control the process. We have plenty of projects and outcomes, but many lack a process.

A great example of simplifying the process is Cheryl Bachelder, who became CEO of Popeyes in 2007. When she took over, the brand was struggling and behind projections for future revenue. One thing she noticed was management and franchisees had over 120 initiatives. Many of them were either redundant or straying away from the most important objectives. So she launched a corporate plan to minimize and refocus these initiatives. She took the company from 120 initiatives to 6. Her focused leadership led to a quadrupled company valuation and over $1 billion in revenue growth over the last 10 years.

Step 3: Create an inner circle. Assemble a group of accountability partners. This is the critical few—the fewer the better. This group completely buys into the process and its stated outcomes. Although they may disagree on how to create a better outcome, they all adhere to the process and are committed to the executables. These are the champions to the process—the folks who truly believe the *why* and *what* of the system. Create roles and lanes for each stakeholder and don't allow outside influences to change the process without consensus first. There's entirely too much noise, information, trends, hacks, and quick fixes to distract us. This inner circle protects you from this noise. It's the best way to filter the noise from the substance.

Step 4: Follow through and keep your head down. It is so easy to get distracted. It is easy to think the grass is greener on the other side. Maybe the competition is moving faster from your vantage point. Maybe you aren't innovating as fast. These are the psychological detours we all must avoid. You establish what you want, create a process, and build an inner circle—that system won't lead you astray. Always be open-minded, curious, and aware of where the market is moving—but all successful strategies are guided by noise-cancelling focus on what really matters.

Practice

A world-class chef needs to experiment with different dishes and practice new techniques in order to perfect his or her craft. When we want to crush a presentation or pitch, we must rehearse, revise, and practice. When it comes to focus, we just expect it to be there, and if it's not, then we must not be able to focus. Stop there. Just like any other skill, attaining focus requires careful practice.

Start by practicing your focus on the little things first. Can you get little wins by focusing for eight seconds, one minute, or even five minutes without a break or distraction? Research has shown that we rekindle childhood curiosity and creativity by focusing on the small details around us. These baby steps add up quickly in the concentration game.

Here's an exercise: Pick a task like lead prospecting, reading an article, or outlining a project. Set a realistic time you can devote to fully engaging in that task. Set your timer, and only perform the set task without breaking for any other distraction. Feel free to silence your phone to avoid any push notifications that might break your concentration. Restrain yourself when you feel the temptation to check your phone or e-mail. Do this for one minute, then five minutes, and see if you can get up to 90 minutes. Ninety minutes is when you should take a break—physically and mentally. When was the last time you went 90 minutes without switching from a task?

Focus on What Actually Matters

Acclaimed leadership expert Andy Stanley interviewed Glen Jackson, cofounder of Jackson Spalding, one of the most trusted and award-winning marketing communication firms in the world. Jackson has worked with some of the world's top organizations. One of the cornerstones to his leadership philosophy is identifying the seven pillars of a preeminent organization. I couldn't help but smile when he mentioned the sixth pillar—fanatical focus:

> This focus provides clarity— clarity of judgment and purpose. Pre-eminent companies do not hesitate to say no to opportunities that just don't make good sense. And they are not distracted by their success. The focus and aim for excellence never waver. Nothing is taken for granted, as they remain humble and hungry, gracious and ambitious. These organizations strive, stretch, strain, and, in persistent fashion, succeed.

"Opportunity does not equal obligation" is a mantra Jackson Spalding takes to heart as an organization. The company is relentless in its determination to consistently deliver results for customers. That mentality persists because it's applied at every level. Any new prospect is thoroughly vetted for all possible future outcomes and possibilities with one overarching question in mind: Do we share mutual business goals and are we building the foundation of a prosperous partnership? If you answer that question honestly when it comes running a business, it really means knowing when to say no.

Wait, you may be thinking—isn't the whole point of this book to increase your capacity and never have to say no? The following mental exercise may help illustrate the contradiction in a clearer way. Pretend you are trapped in a box with a small air pocket at the top. Where do you focus your attention? Probably toward "How the hell do I get out of this box before I suffocate?!" Your neck might as well be locked at a permanent 45-degree angle since you are now utterly fixated on the small sliver of light teasing you. You focus all of your energy upward toward a hopeful escape from the four-walled prison in which you find yourself.

In your panicked frenzy, you never thought to look anywhere else for a possible escape. What's below? You look down and see a bright red arrow pointing straight to an escape hatch. The solutions to our problems are usually in obvious places; we're just too distracted to notice.

Jackson Spalding doesn't let FOMO (fear of missing out) on any opportunity cloud its judgment. The company carefully evaluates each prospect over time and works to cultivate a relationship instead of a simple transaction with their best clients. Don't go chasing every dollar you think you can get. Focus on enhancing the relationships you've already built, and your capacity to do better work will follow.

Jackson Spalding's collective focus is narrow and deep—not wide and shallow. The company also understands the difference between hard-easy and easy-hard. In other words, the organization makes hard decisions when it has to make them—knowing that will make things easier over time—instead of following a take-it-easy approach that only makes things harder over time. Also, preeminent organizations place tremendous focus on teams—not individual talent alone. A healthy organization is about everyone—not just someone.

Focus Directs Performance

As a kid, I (Matt) was diagnosed with ADHD. I displayed dyslexic writing behavior, sometimes using b's instead of d's, or would read a sentence that wasn't actually there. I struggled to pay attention, and sitting still in class was a painfully rare occurrence. Reading and doing homework were my definition of complete and utter torture. I struggled to perform at school; I had mediocre grades, subpar standardized test scores, and consistent worry about my ability to get into a decent college.

Fortunately, my parents never allowed me to use this as a a crutch. I wasn't prescribed Adderall or enrolled in special after-school tutoring programs. I had to learn to pay attention, and I needed to keep up with my classmates. It was excruciatingly hard. My mom tells me I used to pretend I was hot or had a bad rash to get out of finishing my homework. As a child, whenever I was faced with something I didn't want to do, my body and mind invented anything else I'd rather be doing: daydreaming, doodling, fidgeting, and talking to classmates—anything but focusing on the task at hand.

My productivity took an even bigger blow in high school. I distinctly remember when I was a junior in high school taking the ACT and SAT for the first time. I didn't even read the short stories for the English portion and just guessed at the answers. As you could imagine I scored extremely low, my first attempt on the ACT was a 16; 75 percent of other test takers did better. I had to retake the test because my athletic eligibility depended on it. I had to make a 17 or I wouldn't be able to play college golf, a dream on the cusp of reality after four years of tireless practice. My next score wasn't much better; I received just enough to squeak by with an 18. I ultimately graduated high school with a 2.6 GPA. Was this because I wasn't smart, able, or given the right resources? Looking back, I know I could have achieved so much more if I had just found a way to pay more attention and focus on the foundation of learning—engagement.

When we think of people not being able to focus or pay attention or even people diagnosed with ADHD, does this mean they don't have something the rest of us have? If I just wasn't blessed with the focus gene, then how could I stay focused for 18 holes of golf over five hours? What I quickly learned, after sliding into college with a golf scholarship, is that talent or skill has nothing to do with success in life. It is all about intention and having laser-like focus on the most important stuff that doesn't drain you. There was plenty of substance out there for me to dive into and explore further to build my capacity for learning. I had to condition myself to know how to spark engagement when it didn't happen naturally.

This life-altering epiphany only happened after years of challenges and hardships that taught me what I didn't want out of life. Despite repeated failure and defeat, I knew I was destined for more because I knew deep down that I had more to give to the world. Don't you ever wonder how much more you could contribute to society if you cut out the noise and focused on your genuine passions? What if your organization was filled with a thriving network of teams that had the ability to focus on demand?

Now you have the strategy and tactics to start making that dream a reality. The best part about optimizing focus—it creates boundless energy.

Key Point

Focus is a skill; it is the most valuable skill because it is what directs performance. Just because you can't focus now doesn't mean you don't have the ability to later. Practice this skill; it guides everything else in your life.

6 Boundless *Energy* Fuels Performance

Remember, you have only one ride through life so give it all you got and enjoy the ride.
—Jon Gordon, author of *The Energy Bus*

Everything around us is made of energy: light, heat, machines, electricity, sound, and life. Even an object that appears to be solid and still has energy. For the sake of reading this chapter, you don't have to understand quantum physics or know the difference between joules and watts, but you should appreciate that energy is all around us and is a big part of our existence. Essentially, energy is the *capacity* of a physical system to do work.

So, when it comes to human performance or the productivity of an organization, the energy of your people is a big deal. Energy is not only something for the individual; it can take a group of people places they never thought possible. But how do you measure human energy? What is the metric to know if you are operating at your full energy potential? Currently there is no scientific universally accepted way to measure a person's energy level. The only way to measure your energy or the energy of your people is through a subjective view or a personal point of view, for example, "Please rate on a scale of 1–10 . . ." You may be thinking, "My smart watch can!" If this is the case you may want to return your item, because someone sold you a scam.

There is a great saying: "If you don't measure it, it doesn't exist." Another management quote from Peter Drucker is "What gets measured gets managed." Both statements are for the most part true, but they fail with respect to human energy. We can't really measure it objectively and because of this we do a very poor job managing it, but human energy exists nonetheless. When was the last time you had a company meeting and the leadership or management said, "For the next fiscal year our number one KPI is human energy?" You may be laughing or thinking "Yeah, right," but what if human energy was the number one KPI? Heck, it sounds like everything else runs on it.

We don't have the answer to the technology or unit of measure to track human energy, but we will guide you on why it is imperative for the future and how you can manage, sustain, and share it.

For the past five years, we have been working with a health-care company of approximately 11,000 employees. We help improve talent and increase performance through our training platform. They understand that to develop a great culture, you must teach your people how to feel their best. We tackle behavior change, help people find their *why*, and give the foundational methodology to health and performance. During a recent follow-up course, a woman raised her hand and wanted to share a testimonial to the group. She said,

> When I started this training, there was a lot of talk about increasing energy, or feeling better. At the time, I thought I had plenty of energy and was not sure what that meant. After a couple years of incrementally changing habits, I can honestly say I have way more energy than I have ever had and a type of energy I never knew was possible. . . . I truly believe most people don't know they could have more energy or what that would look or feel like because I was in that same boat.

This was a great example of what such elusive energy can do, but also why it is so mismanaged. Nobody can really see it, most aren't tracking it, but it is something we all can feel and notice. Over the next several pages, we want you to imagine if you had more energy potential or if your team or company had more energy potential, what would be possible? If people knew what their true human energy was and what their potential could be, we believe more people would do everything they could to tap into this resource.

Manufactured Energy

There is no denying that we are a society that struggles with energy and yet simultaneously craves it. All you have to do is walk through the airport or a gas station. Everywhere you turn, people are trying to manufacture their energy—energy drinks, coffee, soda pop, sugar, motivational quotes, and stimulants. If you don't feel you have the energy you want or the energy you could have, what are you doing about it? If your organization is not on fire with energy, how are you activating it inside your culture?

Why do we try to manufacture energy, when energy is something that we can naturally harvest for ourselves and our people? How do you create a plan for energy that fuels your passions and desires to live how life is meant to be?

Imagine you have been up all night finalizing the details of the big sales pitch you have tomorrow with Reed, Dune & Associates. You maybe got three good hours of sleep before you awoke to an ear-piercing alarm followed by a bucket of coffee and two pastries from the office lobby. You are greeted by the two partners you are pitching and your team of engineers. It is the biggest pitch of your career; your next promotion relies on it. The positive self-talk is getting old, because you know how fake it is. And even though you prepared like crazy, you still question your internal confidence; you feel energized, but is it real or is it manufactured?

If you rewind the tape, the last four weeks may not have been what you call peak performance. You have caught a cold twice, and you were just told by your doctor that your blood pressure is too high and that you should start your prescription for acid reflux right away. Your sleep apnea is getting worse and you have an appointment with the specialist next week. At work, you are 20 percent behind from projections and you have a customer care issue with a new top customer. You have gained 15 pounds since October of last year, and you don't feel like you can get ahead.

This is normal, right?

As we have spent our time consulting, speaking, and training people within many industries and many demographics, we find this false sense of energy. What is true energy? What does it feel like and how do you sustain it?

We explained that it is difficult to measure energy, but we have subjectively labeled it. Let's look at the different energy levels that we see (Figure 6.1)

Energy Levels (1–10 Scale)

Cooked (0–2). This level of energy is when you just quit; you have nothing more. This is the breaking point. You do not want to get to this point, because this is where nervous breakdowns and severe health issues occur. At this point you physically and mentally cannot go any farther.

Lethargic (2–5). At this level you have chronic fatigue. Most organizations have many people operating at this level of

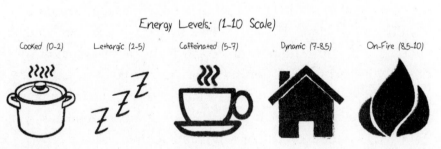

FIGURE 6.1 Energy potential.

energy. This is the level that doesn't happen overnight, but only gets better if you get off the train that brought you here.

Caffeinated (5–7). There isn't much description needed; we have all run into these people and are not sure if they are machines that are short circuiting or people who needed one less cappuccino. Caffeinated energy is how many people try to manufacture their energy. When they are not on an upper, they are most likely on snooze.

Dynamic (7–8.5). Now we are getting places. These are the folks who have control over their energy. They don't rely on outside factors or influences to produce energy; they have a basic understanding of protecting and building their commodity of energy. They get the job done with enthusiasm and happiness. The only limiting factor is they don't always sustain it.

On Fire (8.5–10). We all have been here, but most don't know how to stay or get back here. This isn't the external energy that many of us think about; this is the internal energy that fuels us to do everything necessary. When we are on fire and people know it, they feel it, and the work speaks for itself. You have it and have a true understanding of how to repeat it. At this point energy isn't something that you even have to worry about and you can tap into it when needed—your energy capacity is large.

Energy fuels the performance of your organization, and the great news is it is contagious. The bad news is lack of energy or the wrong energy is contagious as well. The difference between sustained energy and manufactured energy is so drastic that once you develop the sustained on-fire energy you will never want to let it go. Let us show you how to protect your people's energy and give you tips to enhance it.

Three Tips for Protecting Energy inside Your Organization

1. Allow Autonomy

When was the last time you were at the Department of Motor Vehicles? Let's take a ride down memory lane to visualize the collective energy of this place. Long lines, poor customer service, and the burning desire to get out of there as fast as you can. What is the energy of the people working? What was your energy like while waiting for your number to be called? Some might consider the DMV one of the most un-autonomous entities in our country and you feel it with no emotion, no smiles, no laughter, just transactions, and everyone's energy suffers because of it.

The first rule to protecting your people's energy is to allow people to find their rhythm and have autonomy. If people need to take breaks, let them take breaks; if somebody is more creative working from 7:00 a.m. to 3:00 p.m., make it happen. We all have different rules and systems, but as our work evolves from manual labor to brain power, it is important to understand that people are not robots, they need to find their true rhythm.

2. Create More Human Connection

Virtual meetings, e-mails, texts, SMS, computers, and social platforms are used more and more every day. This has helped tremendously to globalize the world. We can now connect to coworkers, vendors, and friends all over the world and at any time.

To protect your people's energy, try to create structured or encouraged opportunities to connect in person. Company reunions, team-building projects, and daily or weekly huddles all promote face-to-face interaction and energy. Think about it as the difference between watching a live concert streaming from your living room or being at the concert in the middle of the action. They are ultimately the same thing on the surface, but the experience and value are exponentially different. The data shows that not only are we texting a conversation that in the past we had over coffee, but only 25 percent of people actually get a phone call during the week. Bring the human element back to the office; your people's energy will thank you.

3. Stop Offering It

One of the biggest factors zapping people's energy is unhealthy food: cookies, cake, ice cream, fried foods, free soda/pop, and candy. One of the biggest mistakes for companies in this arena is making it so easy to eat these unhealthy things. When you are thinking about the purpose of your organization, don't take for granted the little things you do that may seem harmless, but over time create energy vacuums. Providing treats and candy is not the problem. Creating a culture that expects and demands them is the problem. We have experience helping organizations clean up their free snack and beverage options in a way that encourages good choices and helps elevate sustainable energy, verses squandering it. People love upgrades. Don't just say we are getting rid of the junk food; bring in options that make people happy, healthy, and energized!

Five Keys to Building Your Energy

1. Water

Drink more water. Water is needed for two things: cleansing the body and boosting energy. When people are low on energy, it probably means they are not drinking enough water. Ideally, we should drink half our body weight in ounces of water per day.

2. Sleep

Think of sleep as a charger—like the charger to your phone. To fully fuel or charge you need seven to eight hours of sleep. You also need a basic routine that allows you to transition to sleep and maintain the same sleep pattern. If you feel that your mind is tired or you need a quick refresh, don't hesitate to take a nap, but limit it to 15–20 minutes max. This is our secret weapon. (We love to nap.)

3. Nutrition

Superfoods are nutrient-dense foods, that pack a lot of bang in each bite. Chlorophyll is a key nutrient for energy. Foods high in chlorophyll (green foods), include wheatgrass, spirulina/chlorella, kale, spinach, and broccoli can be extremely effective for improving and sustaining your energy.

4. Movement

On days we don't move we tend to have the lowest energy. This could be during travel, writing, or busy days of meetings. Ten to 15 minutes of movement is like 24 hours of recharge. Find the time to move daily.

5. No Stimulants

Don't use stimulants like soda pop, coffee, energy drinks, sugary drinks, supplements, or drugs for energy. If you are consuming something for the quick effects and the outcome of having greater energy, this is the stimulant we are talking about. If you like to drink coffee or drink the occasional soda, this is not a problem. Change the mindset that energy comes from a can, bottle, or pill; true energy doesn't.

Bonus: Recharge, Recover, and Reward

The bonus for building energy is something we call *white space*. In Chapter 8 you will read more about all the ideas for white space, like meditation, massage, listening to soft music. Think of white space as your personal strategy to recharge, recover, and reward yourself. The critical part for maximizing whitespace is finding something that works for you and something that can become a ritual. This bonus is not only a key for building energy, but if you implement white space in your life you will start to see a competitive advantage.

Keep the Juice Flowing

When you think of commodities, what do you think about? Crude oil, coffee, cotton, corn, cattle, natural gas, gold, silver, and sugar? These are currently some of the top traded commodities in the world. Commodities are raw materials or products that are considered the same no matter who produces them. Some people now consider insurance to be a commodity, due to the basic coverage being the same across many different companies and the only thing that differs is the price. We all know that when it comes to commodities, you want to buy low and sell high; nobody likes paying more for something if they don't have to. The one truth is that all commodities are considered either useful or valuable. The value of these commodities goes up as the demands get higher and supply gets smaller.

Throughout this book, we have made the point that human demands are increasing and human capacity is shrinking. This is the basic equation for a commodity value increase. But when it comes to humans, what are our commodities? What do we produce that is useful and valuable, and how do we pay for it? What are the costs? It's fun to look at the most expensive commodities by weight. White truffles cost close to $2,000/pound, gold is $1,300/ounce, and diamonds are $13,000/carat. In the 1630s, there was such a demand for tulips that it created tulip mania in the Netherlands. Tulips ended up costing more than houses for a short period of time, but shortly after this boom they had an epic fall that caused a financial crash. It's fascinating to watch goods that we consider to be useful and valuable, and how over the years their usefulness and value goes up and down.

When it comes to humans, *energy* is the commodity that is now trading higher and higher and will only continue to get more valuable. Now some might say, *time* is our most precious commodity. We agree; time is something that all of us have a limited supply of. But when it comes to time, it comes down to two factors: (1) you only get so much time, and (2) your time is more valuable when you have more energy. So, in terms of what you should protect and value, first it is your energy, because when you have this, you end up making better use of your time. The cost of energy is priceless. Everyone has the same amount of time, but not everyone has the same amount of energy. There is a finite amount of time, there isn't a finite amount of energy. It is not about spending more time doing things; it is the energy you put in to those things.

Energy *fuels* performance and your life!

Key Point

Energy is your most precious commodity. Energy is the fuel to performance. We want you to build your energy, we want you to protect your energy, and most importantly, we want you to share your energy.

energy + passion = *drive*

7 Unstoppable *Drive* Propels Performance

Human beings have an innate inner drive to be autonomous, self-determined, and connected to one another. And when that drive is liberated, people achieve more and live richer lives.
—Daniel Pink, author of *Drive*

Finding the Pot of Gold?

When you were growing up, do you remember driving down the road after a rainstorm and seeing a large, beautiful, colorful rainbow? Did your parents tell you there was a pot of gold at the end of the rainbow? As you continued driving, you may have noticed that the rainbow never gets any closer; you can see it, but you can't ever touch it. Rainbows appear to form perfectly rounded arches, but in reality, rainbows form full circles. When you're standing on the ground, you can see the light that's reflected by the raindrops above the horizon. Thus, you can't see a rainbow's lower or hidden half, unless you are in a plane, in a helicopter, or possibly on a tall mountain top. Since a rainbow is a circle, you'll never reach the end. Rainbows seem to move when you do, because the light that forms the rainbow is always at a specific distance and angle from you. Rainbows are optical illusions, and that's why you'll never find that pot of gold!

What is the meaning of the pot of gold at the end of the rainbow? Is it wealth, success, fulfillment, happiness, the possibility that all your hopes and dreams may come true if you find that pot of gold? This chapter is about learning how to have greater motivation and the drive to move mountains for you or your organization. For many organizations and their people, having the motivation and drive to perform at their best can be as elusive as a rainbow. To get to the pot of gold, we first have to create laser focus, which creates a clear path or direction. Once we settle on the direction, we then fuel up for the journey with boundless energy. Given that we have plenty of fuel it is only natural to unleash what we believe can propel you to accomplish anything you set your mind to. This pot of gold is what's called *drive* or intrinsic motivation, and it's something that organizations have been trying to figure out for a long time.

What would you say has changed most about work over the last 30 years? Is it the automation or globalization? Is it the blurred lines of work and life? Maybe it's the fact that we can work remotely and don't even have to be in a physical office? These tectonic cultural shifts have changed not only the nature of work, but why we work in the first place, our inner *drive*.

With the influx of millennials entering the workforce, organizations are scrambling to attract and motivate this group. This generation grew up in an era defined by instant access to data, automated workflows, and hundreds of different ways to solve the same problem. They don't want to be told how to do something; they want to show you a better, faster way to solve a problem. This means that traditional command-and-control-style corporate structures, with layers upon layers of processes, rules, and regulations only stifle creativity and impede innovation. Autonomy and meaning are the new engines that drive this next generation.

This isn't a novel concept. Every generation has had differences. Consider when Jack Welch was named CEO of General Electric in 1981; he could sense the coming change. He was eager to tackle a seemingly impossible task: Create a small-business culture at one of the world's largest multinational conglomerates. Fierce global competition and consolidation created the sense of urgency he needed to turn this ship around, and it required people to embrace rapid change as an opportunity for growth instead of an imminent threat. His now legendary Work-Out model was built on three foundational pillars for driving performance:

1. Simplicity—Remove the layers of complexity and communicate a clear strategy for growth so each person knows exactly what added value means to the organizational purpose.
2. Speed—Reorganize teams around subject matter experts who have the intellectual authority and self-assurance to make quicker decisions and the ability to act faster.
3. Self-reliance—Be willing to let your people make mistakes because failure is the best teacher.

By the time Welch retired in 2001, General Electric's overall valuation had increased over 4,000 percent. This remarkable turnaround was driven by a singular goal: for each of the 14 core business units to be number one or two globally. Once you filter out all the distractions and focus on the reality of what needs to be done, the sky is truly the limit. He gave his people what we all desire—absolute assurance in our ability to shape the future by driving meaningful change.

The final piece to the performance engine and your competitive advantage is getting people to want to do it because they want to do it, not because you told them to do it. Creating inner *drive* has always been important, but you can't start with *drive*. Inner drive is deployed when you set your people up for success. If you want inner *drive* in your people, teach them how to focus, provide an environment that creates energy, and watch how this combination will take your organization and your people to places they never thought possible while simultaneously leaving the competition in the dust.

Motivation: Intrinsic versus Extrinsic

Imagine if your entire organization were fully engaged and highly motivated on a consistent basis; what kind of outcomes would you see? Consider that almost 70 percent of the workforce is not engaged in what they do, you can assume most are also not intrinsically motivated. Maybe you're asking, yeah, but what motivates people? How do you ensure people are driven and engaged? How do I motivate myself? How do I get my team or organization motivated? Understanding what engages and motivates people and their organizations is the trillion-dollar question we all are chasing. Let us start with the two types of motivation.

There are two types of motivation we all experience daily—extrinsic, or external, and intrinsic, or internal. Let's start with extrinsic motivation, or the carrot and the stick. Extrinsic motivation can be extremely powerful in the beginning, especially for simple tasks and in the right situations. Maybe you watch an inspiring movie, attend a conference and listen to a powerful motivational speaker, hire a personal trainer to get you into better shape, bring in games to the workplace, or receive a bonus or pay raise—these are all examples of extrinsic motivation.

The best example of extrinsic motivation occurs in the weight-loss industry. The weight loss industry is a $50 billion-a-year industry with a 95 percent failure rate and most of it is based on quick, easy fixes. Obesity is at an all-time high around the world and has become a huge problem in our society. Today we have greater access to health-care services, information, gyms, diet plans, and highly trained health professionals, but we are still losing the obesity battle.

Most people start down their weight loss journey with the expectation that this is it—this is my time, and I am going to lose weight once and for all. You are jacked up and ready to take on the world, but slowly extrinsic motivation begins to wane and eventually disappears. Most people feel like they have failed and most have failed because they lost their motivation. This may be true—but what they had lost was extrinsic or external motivation. What if there were a much more powerful and sustainable motivation that could be learned to drive lasting results?

Over the course of the past 30 years, almost everything has changed, yet organizations are still over-relying on extrinsic, or external carrot-and-stick, motivators to get ahead. We must recognize that extrinsic motivation has its place, but if you truly want to create significant, sustainable change, intrinsic or internal motivation is an exponentially more powerful way to tackle the complex world we live in today.

> There's a mismatch between what science knows and what business does.
>
> —Daniel Pink, author of *Drive*

Daniel Pink's quote and research illustrate how much evidence there is in the power of intrinsic or internal motivation, but most of the world still relies on external motivation because of the quick response and ease of execution. Intrinsic motivation is a process that takes time to develop but creates extremely powerful results.

Chris's Story

When I first entered the health and fitness industry over 30 years ago, I was all about giving people information: take flaxseeds, coconut oil, cod liver oil, wheatgrass, and spirulina/chlorella; engage in strength training; and so on. But I slowly learned information alone in most cases does not create sustainable change. In 1990 I was hired as the director of fitness and personal training at one of the largest health clubs in the world—the Michigan Athletic Club (MAC). The MAC was massive facility, with over 275,000 square feet of courts, pools, and the latest and greatest fitness equipment.

My number-one role at the club was to help build a large, vibrant, personal training program. In the beginning business was good; we had many wonderful personal trainers, along with a large membership base.

After only a few short years, however, business began to stagnate, and there was a growing sense a frustration among many of our trainers. Our personal trainers were getting frustrated with many of their clients due to the lack of results. The clients had hired their trainer with a variety of goals in mind, but, in many cases, did not follow through with the trainers' advice. For example, many members sought advice to improve their back health; decrease hip, knee, or shoulder pain; or improve their type 2 diabetes, blood pressure, or acid reflux, but seldom followed the trainers' recommendations. They said they wanted to increase their strength, but seldom came to the gym. They said they wanted to lose weight but were not willing to follow the nutrition and fitness plan their trainer laid out for them. Most of our clients did a great job in the presence of their trainer, but when the trainer was not watching, their motivation or drive seemed to be on vacation. Our trainers would say, "My clients just don't have the drive or motivation to follow the plan to reach the goals they are asking for." Why were our clients not motivated to reach their goals? Why were they not driven to follow through on the advice of their trainer? What was missing? How could we help them achieve greater results? Did they lack discipline? Where they not in line when willpower was handed out?

As a team, we decided it was time to take a new direction. We discussed our goals, vision, and mission. We all believed the information we were sharing with our clients was solid, but when it came to helping our clients learn how to stay motivated we were missing something. We all agreed that for our trainers to be more successful and for our program to grow and prosper, we had to do a better job motivating our clients. Extrinsic, or external, motivation was the primary motivation strategy we had been using, but this type of motivation was not powerful enough to get the results we were all looking for. It was time for our entire team to learn intrinsic, motivational skills.

We began our process by digging deeper into our client's expectations. What did our clients truly want? We changed from giving information and relying on our external rewards to educating and focusing on people's desires or purpose. Then we began helping each client learn how to enjoy the process of getting healthy and in better shape; this unlocked their internal drive. Slowly, one by one, our entire team of trainers learned the process and the power of intrinsic motivation. In return, our clients started getting better results than ever before and were having more fun along the way. The word around our community began to spread. More and more members and nonmembers entered our program; they could see the movement and wanted to learn the magic. Physicians around the community started referring more and more of their patients to our program, and within one year our program revenues doubled. Our clients were having fun and getting great results, our trainers were fully engaged and our business exploded into one of the top revenue-producing personal training programs in the country.

Changing behavior can be extremely challenging—actually if it isn't hard, there is probably little change happening. The key for creating sustainable change is creating repeatable habits that grow into daily rituals. If you follow the most successful people, they all have daily rituals that are congruent with their goals.

Learning the Intrinsic Motivation Process

What *do you want?*

If you don't have a crystal-clear goal or expectation, it is hard to create a plan, and it is impossible to measure success.

Why *do you want this?*

Many people want to lose weight, get into better shape, be more successful, or make more money. These are very clear and attainable, but if you aren't committed or truly aware of why you want it, the chances of getting there are very low. When you discover your *why* or purpose, you have the ammo to reach those goals.

Building Habits *into* Rituals

If you were asked, "What shoe did you put on first today?" what would you say? Do you put the right shoe on first? Do you have no clue what shoe went on first, but if you look down, you see two shoes? Did you know that 80–90 percent of what we do each and every day are unconscious habits—habits we don't even think about. Taking a shower, getting dressed, brushing your teeth, drinking a cup of coffee or eating breakfast, driving to work—we are all just a bunch of habits. Building new habits takes focus and energy, and they need to be built one at a time. This makes it easy to start and easy to implement. As your habits get stronger over time they slowly turn into rituals for life.

Enjoy the Process

Think back on the most rewarding parts of your life. Maybe it was a major renovation project or finally earning a law degree while working a full-time job. Whatever your proudest accomplishment may be, they all seem to have one common theme—they were hard or challenging.

The best moments in life aren't reached by taking shortcuts. They aren't reached by pushing the easy button. The best moments in life are usually filled with failure and seemingly impossible obstacles you had to overcome. The end goal or ambition kept you going through the rough patches along the way.

At On Target Living, our role is not to take a prescriptive approach or tell people exactly what to do; our role is to trigger behavior change and help to create a process that people can execute, manage, and enjoy. Whatever habit you are trying to improve, begin by asking better questions. If your goal is to have greater health, what do you need to know more of? How can you move your body daily or what foods can you replace with healthier options? Enjoy the process. Intrinsic motivation can be transferred into almost any area of your life that you want to improve.

We receive many questions about wanting to write a book; we believe everyone has a book in them. Did you know that approximately 98 percent of people who begin writing a book never complete it? Just like starting a weight-loss program most people begin the writing process with great excitement, but slowly this excitement begins to disappear. Writing your first book can be challenging and even frustrating at times. The writing process may feel like your first business suit: stiff and uncomfortable. You may wonder, "How do I translate talking points to the page in a creative way? How do I find a compelling way to hook the reader right away? Do people really want to read what I have to say?" You start to avoid the writing process because it is hard and unpleasant. At this point, you have two options: stop and give up, or change your thinking. What do you want? What is your purpose, your *why*, for writing your book? How can you enjoy the process of writing? Here are a few questions to ask yourself and can be translated for any process:

- Why am I writing this book in the first place?
- Who's the audience and what do I want to communicate above all else?
- When's the ideal time for me to focus and write?
- How can I get myself in the best frame of mind for this type of work?
- What's the most rewarding part about creating something from scratch?

Create a writing process and environment that is enjoyable. Maybe it's candles for soft ambient light, classical music at a low volume, and meditation before each writing session. The writing process can be challenging and sometimes difficult, but it can also be pleasant and extremely gratifying with the proper intrinsic motivation mindset. This creates plenty of energy and passion to devote to other endeavors because you finally have a platform to start connecting with exponentially more people than ever before. You are now telling yourself a different story; you have learned how to enjoy the process and journey instead.

These simple questions allowed us to help others build a plan that they were driven to do (Figure 7.1).

Staying motivated when nobody is looking is what we all should strive for. How do you build habits throughout an entire organization? How do you create a culture of highly driven people?

If you can build intrinsically motivated people, you will win much more.

Don't rely on information and the carrot-and-stick approach. Educate your people on how to achieve their desires and help them unlock why they want those desires. This will lead to better habits that turn into rituals, and rituals are what truly drive people to do the right thing day in and day out.

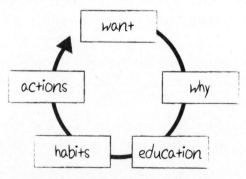

FIGURE 7.1 Intrinsic motivation model.

Do it because you want to, not because you have to.

Here is a funny story from Chris about why a prescriptive approach to almost anything is difficult to sustain. Ideally your goal is to build habits that are yours or your people's. You must make mistakes, experiment, and make it your own.

One time I was out to dinner with a group of people who were attending one of my training sessions through their company's leadership and development event. I love eating baked potatoes and sweet potatoes (Matt may say to a fault!). During this dinner outing, I ordered an entrée off the menu and asked if I could get a plain baked potato with a side of olive oil. The rest of the party ordered the exact same thing as if it was one of the restaurant's signature dishes. You should have seen the waiter's face! He looked at us like we had just landed from Mars. "Sir, we don't have any potatoes here. This is a sushi restaurant."

Resiliency

It's not what you *know*; it's what you *do*!

It is impossible to talk about *drive* without mentioning resiliency. To be resilient or to have resiliency, you must have internal drive to push through the chaos. When we work with companies, the word *resilience* comes up an awful lot. They say things like "We need to help our people become more resilient" or "We think our weakness is our lack of resiliency in our people." What they are really saying is "We need our people to be able to adapt, recover, and act in a way that keeps us moving forward no matter what."

The economy and market place have become extremely volatile and competitive. This has caused an increase in the need for organizations, teams, and leaders, to have more hustle, show a level of grit and resiliency, and have that inner hunger for success. We all need to have that positive attitude that gets us through obstacles and setbacks, yet only 17 percent of business leaders report being confident they have the right leadership capabilities to execute their strategy.

If you are looking to build a resilient culture, shift away from giving people only what they want and give them what they need. We know kids love to eat candy and stay up late, but these don't help them do better in school or athletics. If we think about how we teach our kids, we can start to teach our people how to strive for the outcomes of the future.

Just because your kids don't like eating fruits and vegetables, brushing their teeth, or going to bed early doesn't mean these things won't benefit them in the long run. With the talent shortage that many organizations have, we have noticed an urgency to attract the best talent. This urgency usually leads to the easy solution of giving people those external quick rewards that fail to build resilient and driven cultures.

Create a process that will attract the right talent and a process that will grow and keep the right talent. If you attract talent but can't retain the talent, there is no way you can build a resilient culture.

Move Your Body

We are expected to manage ourselves more than ever before—not just managing our time, but the overall strategy and execution of what we think are the most important goals for our respective roles. Your superiors rely on your knowledge and specialized expertise to pilot the day-to-day execution. This requires self-management with a major emphasis on the self. If we aren't being ordered what to do, how do we know what to prioritize and commit our time and effort toward? Due to this self-management, there will be some days where you just don't have the motivation. So outside of tapping into your internal drive and building a process, how can you trigger motivation?

Here is a kick start if you need some instant motivation. Harvard social psychologist Amy Cuddy discussed motivation in her TED Talk. Her research was on how physical movement like pumping your arms, dancing around, puffing up your chest, and verbalizing can be extremely motivating to the mind. We have always believed that the mind motivates the body, but through Amy Cuddy's work along with many others', we now know that the body can motivate the mind—you just need to get up and move. If you are feeling stuck, in a rut, or like you just don't have the juice, start moving the body and your physiology will begin to change. In return, your psychology will also begin to change— your mood will be enhanced, cognition and mental productivity will improve, and you will enjoy greater focus, energy, and drive. Next time you need a shot of motivation, get moving; motion creates positive emotion! We will discuss movement more in depth in Chapter 10.

Building a foundation of work and life on inner *drive* will rarely lead you astray. Your organization will be able to withstand all market conditions because these behaviors allow you to seize the immense opportunity change brings. You will start manufacturing ideas instead of just finished goods. You will attract the best talent because they already believe in your purpose and know they will be challenged to help bring it to life. *Drive* is something we all are seeking and, as you can see, we all innately have; the real art is creating a process that brings it out of people. Maybe we can find the pot of gold at the end of the rainbow.

The last three chapters helped you see what it takes to expand capacity—*focus, energy, drive*. Now, let's go after the foundation that makes it all possible: *REST, EAT, MOVE.*

FIGURE 7.2 The three performance outcomes of building capacity.

Key Point

Drive is your internal motivation to succeed and the propeller to life.

8   *REST*

Building your foundation for greater capacity begins with getting enough *REST*. In this chapter, we will show you how to achieve optimal recovery and why it is critical for greater performance for you and your organization.

Imagine waking up after a restful night's sleep full of energy and a clear mind. How would you feel? How would you perform? Imagine having a plan that could help you feel this way on a consistent basis.

As our world continues to speed up, it becomes increasingly challenging to balance life's priorities. Work, family, and friends are always one click or swipe away. We are all more connected, and the demands of living life in hyperdrive leave less time for self-care. As we try to do more, the necessity for rest increases.

We have worked with many organizations that believed working long hours, with little sleep, and a heavy workload was the only way to get ahead. We all must work hard to achieve our goals, but better performance does not require grinding people into dust.

Many organizations believe rest is a soft or optional prerequisite for employee productivity and performance: "We know we need to get more rest"; (and here comes their *but*) "maybe we will get to that when we hit our other targets." Rarely do organizations look at more recovery as a strategy to improve performance. But when we hear from executives about their people just going through the motions or having a deer-in-the-headlights look when they ask them to think critically, it's usually a symptom of not getting enough rest. Let's start implementing better recovery strategies by understanding stress.

Stress

Have you heard of stress? When we ask this question at our events, everyone begins to laugh and roll their eyes a little. Everyone has experienced some type of stress in their life—physical stress, emotional stress, and financial stress to name just a few. Stressors come in all shapes and sizes and are lurking around every corner, but do we truly understand stress and how it can break us and our organizations down? We believe when people and organizations begin to understand stress, and its impact on the bottom line, they begin to understand the need to have rest and rejuvenation strategies in place to help control it. The Centers for Disease Control and Prevention state unequivocally that 80 percent of our medical expenditures are now stress related.[1] Not only is stress breaking us down from a health and medical standpoint; it is also breaking us down on the performance side, due to lack of focus, energy, and drive.

Mindset 1: Stress Is What You Say to Yourself!

Over 2,000 years ago, the great philosopher Epictetus stated:

> People are not disturbed by things, but the view they take of them. It's not what happens to you but how you react to it! Pain and suffering comes from the stories we tell ourselves about the future. We cannot choose our external circumstances, but we can choose how to respond to them.

[1] https://www.cdc.gov/chronicdisease/overview/index.htm#ref17

His wisdom is as profound today as it was 2,000 years ago. We don't need to squash every little stressor that we encounter each day—we just need to control our response to them. We manufacture most stress from our primal fear of the unknown and assume the worst. Stressors are past or future threats that don't actually exist in the now. If a bear barrels across a field toward you (Figure 8.1), that is a true threat—you should *run*! But if you start to get chronic hypertension because of the demands of your job, that is a perceived threat you create for yourself.

Stress is a fact of life, and everyone will experience a major crisis at some point. One of our good friends and colleagues, Phil Nuernberger, PhD, a leading expert in the world on stress and working with the mind, has truly educated the On Target Living team on how powerful the mind can be in controlling stress. He believes it's not about good or bad stress; it is about creating balance and harmony. If you are an overstimulated person, you

FIGURE 8.1 Is the bear real or not?

will need more rest. If you are an understimulated person, you will need more activity. Dr. Phil says we think of stress as only arousal (overstimulation) and a lot of it is, but many people handle stress by just stopping everything or completely shutting down (understimulation). We all need arousal, and we all need withdrawal, but if there is imbalance we create stress. Dr. Phil calls the mind an instrument, and he says we all need proper skills to control our instrument.

Most people think of stress as psychological. Stress is not worry, frustration, or anxiety—all of these emotions may be a response to stress, but they are not stress. Stress is physiological: heart rate, muscular activity, hormonal function, and digestion are the main physical responses to stress. Many stress resources explain how fight or flight, or rest and digest, are automatic responses, meaning you have little control over your stress response. That may be true in some cases, like running into a bear or almost getting into a car accident, but how about speaking in front of a large crowd, being under the gun with an important deadline, or having a tough meeting with one of your colleagues? Is it possible to control your response to to these fears or threats? Most people and organizations believe stress is out of their control. They have little control over their daily circumstances, and stress is just going to hit them at any time. Here is what you need to know: The human body was designed to cope with stress. Imminent threats to survival aren't melting organizations and its people down today. It is the perception of threat and the distorted reactions that take their toll. Deadlines, conflicts, demands, teamwork, financial responsibilities—it is the perceived death by a thousand cuts that is draining our capacity and beating us down. But it doesn't have to be that way; we have control over our reactions.

Can you imagine if you had to think about your heart beating or taking a breath while you were sleeping? The human body is truly amazing with all its connected systems and processes. One of the most remarkable systems is the autonomic nervous system. The autonomic nervous system acts as a stress control center in the body; regulating the heart, digestion, respiratory rate, perspiration, pupil dilation, sexual arousal, and many organs and muscles. The autonomic nervous system is always working to maintain balance with our internal systems. Whereas most of the actions of the autonomic nervous system are involuntary, some such as breathing and heart rate work in tandem with the conscious mind. It is possible to learn how to control many areas of the human body through the conscious mind. With a little practice, you can learn how to control many areas of the human body that affect your health and performance.

The autonomic nervous system is divided into two parts—the sympathetic nervous system (SNS) and the parasympathetic nervous system (PNS). The job of the autonomic nervous system is to synchronize both systems and maintain balanced responses throughout the body.

SNS: Gas Pedal—"Fight or Flight"

The sympathetic nervous system is the gas pedal—this is what most people think stress is. You see or feel a threat, the alarm goes off, and the entire body goes into high alert with all hands on deck! Your heart rate goes up, pupils dilate, blood pressure rises, perspiration increases, muscles contract, and digestion stops. You can't have healthy digestion when the SNS is overactivated! Healthy digestion means you have the ability to break down food and absorb it.

Remember, it does not matter if the threat is real or perceived—it is all about your reaction. Fight or flight can help us perform at a high level for short periods of time, but the chronic sympathetic dominance breaks us down physically and mentally. This is what we call the bear response.

PNS: The Brake—"Rest and Digest"

If the sympathetic nervous system is the five-alarm fire, then the parasympathetic nervous system is laying in a hammock drinking a piña colada. Think of the sympathetic nervous system as the throttle and the parasympathetic nervous system as the brake. Heart rate and blood pressure drops, nerves calm, brain waves slow down, muscles relax, vessels dilate, digestion increases, and your pupils constrict. Rest and digest helps us calm down and relax for extended periods of time, but chronic parasympathetic dominance depletes and atrophies the mind and body. This is what we call the *possum response.*

Sympathetic and parasympathetic divisions typically function in opposition to each other, but both systems are essentially working together to create harmony within the body. The parasympathetic nervous system slows everything down, promoting a rest-and-digest response. It sounds like we all need more of the parasympathetic nervous system in our lives—and yes, we probably do! But more and more people are allowing their parasympathetic nervous system to become too dominant. We begin to lose muscle tone, depression and withdrawal begin to creep in, and many times we feel a level of emotional flatness. We start to lose interest in our passions and procrastinate on doing anything constructive. We begin to sleep too much and don't feel like getting out of bed. We are tired all of the time and start to feel like we have lost our juice for living. One of the most powerful methods to get people back into balance from a dominant parasympathetic nervous system is movement. Movement stimulates the sympathetic nervous system and speeds things up to get the mind and body back into balance.

With the sympathetic nervous system speeding things up, it begins to promote a fight-or-flight response. This is essential in small amounts for you to show up and crush it every day. You can show up with focus and energy to present your ideas with gusto at the morning presentation. But as many of us have seen throughout our society, this 24/7/365 overstimulation forces us into an unsustainable overdrive. Chronic dominance of the sympathetic nervous system, or bear response, starts to overstimulate our nerves and we become increasingly aggressive and impulsive. Blood pressure rises, inflammation goes haywire, muscles become sore, the mind is distracted, and digestion suffers. You are always on edge, agitated, and rarely sleep well. Rest and rejuvenation begin to quiet the sympathetic activity, transitioning you to a more parasympathetic response. The fastest way to trigger the parasympathetic nervous system is using the diaphragm to breathe; this is called diaphragmatic breathing, or belly breathing. We will discuss this later in the chapter.

If you slam on the brakes, you will eventually need to hit the gas. If you are just wide open on the gas, eventually you will need the brakes. Figure 8.2 shows you how to respond based on your stress reactions. Remember stress is ultimately what you tell yourself or, in this case, how you react.

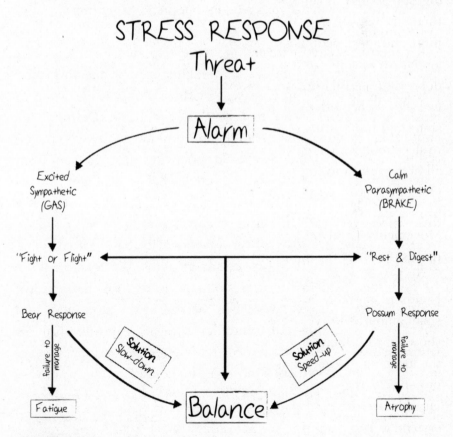

FIGURE 8.2 Stress response.

Mindset 2: It Is the Lack of Recovery That Is Breaking Us Down!

The first half of conquering stress is controlling your reaction to stress and understanding the difference between real and perceived forms of stress. However, positive self-talk, belly breathing, and good reactions don't always cut it. The other half to this coin is implementing small periods of rest throughout your day.

Most people who know my dad, Chris Johnson, consider him an eternal optimist. The glass of life is always half full from his vantage point. He is always portraying a positive outlook on life and situations, and making people around him feel better about themselves. This attitude can take you a long way as discussed earlier. But Mr. Positive can't always rely on that tactic to get him through every situation.

Recently he shared with me his travel experience coming back from Hong Kong. He conducted a weeklong course and was ready to come home. His trip consisted of three stops: Hong Kong to Seoul, South Korea; Seoul to Seattle; and Seattle to Detroit. This around-the-world trip is part of the job, and like many who travel, can become normal and very manageable. But this trip went from tough to miserable. With a five-hour delay before his flight to Seattle, Dad and the rest of the passengers were starting to lose it a little. It was very early, nothing was open, and there was nowhere to sleep to take the edge off the 11-hour trip that awaited them. Most people on this flight just laid down across the concrete floor, ate junk food, watched movies, and complained for the next five hours. Dad was just as stressed as the rest of the passengers and knew belly breathing and mindfulness wasn't going to slay this colossal stress monster. He noticed that there was a spa that opened at 6:00 a.m. and if you got a massage you could also take a shower. For the next hour, he relaxed with a nice massage and a rejuvenating shower, with the last 30 seconds being cold. The next leg of his journey went from unbearably dreadful to positively pleasant.

There's always a creative solution to manage stress—you just have to look in the right places.

We can learn a great deal from the rigorous training program of the United States Navy's primary Special Operations Team, the Navy SEALs (Sea, Air, and Land). The SEALs are an elite fighting team that works under extremely high levels of stress. What is fascinating about the Navy SEAL training is how quickly they break down potential SEAL candidates. After only a few hours, days, or weeks, 75–80 percent of the SEAL candidates have dropped or washed out of the program. Most of the candidates were extremely motivated, many were extremely strong and in great shape, but one by one the SEAL instructors broke them down with merciless efficiency. How do the SEAL instructors do it? *Stress!*

The SEALs know if you load up on stress and take away ample recovery, most people will crack and want to give up. The SEAL instructors deprived candidates of sleep, sometimes allowing them as little as two to three hours a night; limited their food and water; and created an extremely uncomfortable environment. They also put the candidates' bodies through an exhausting regimen of running, swimming, and climbing through inhospitable conditions. On top of this extremely demanding physical stress, the emotional stress was even greater—threats to SEAL candidate survival were everywhere and many of the candidates actually believed this gauntlet of pain would kill them, and truth be told, it could! Why are the Navy SEALs looked upon as one of the elite fighting organizations in the world? *Capacity!* The Navy SEALs have immense capacity to handle stress. They can handle almost anything that comes their way without diminishing their performance.

One area we found extremely interesting in the Navy SEAL training is that candidates who possessed a strong *purpose*—a powerful *why*—had the greatest chances of becoming a Navy SEAL. This can also be said for the most successful organizations. A strong purpose is forged from the resilience of experience and wisdom. In most organizations, the amount of stress is nothing like Navy SEAL training. But over time, drip by drip, stress can and will take its toll on our health and performance. The most effective antidote for chronic stress is rest and rejuvenation; it will allow you to weather any storm that comes your way.

Hormonal Balance

Before we jump into the *rest* and *rejuvenation* strategies and tactics, we need to discuss one more critical physiological factor impacted by stress—your hormones. Persistent weight gain, increased belly fat, loss of muscle, low libido, fatigue, anxiety, irritability, depression, poor sleep, sweating, cravings, and poor digestion are problems for both men and women that may be due to unbalanced hormonal levels. We all need to step back and ask better questions: Why are our hormones out of balance? What may be causing this epidemic of hormonal challenges? Could it be that our fast-paced and demanding lifestyles are starting to break us down faster than our bodies can keep up?

What Is a Hormone?

Hormones are chemical messengers that coordinate physiology and behavior, by regulating, integrating, and controlling our bodily functions. Think of your hormonal system as a beautiful orchestra, all working hard to bring balance and harmony to the mind and body. Hormones, like other systems in the body, are affected by stress. When most people think of hormones, they generally think of sex hormones or steroidal hormones, which regulate metabolism, inflammation, immune function, salt and water balance, sexual characteristics, and the ability to fight off illness and heal the body.

The volume of questions we receive surrounding hormones has exploded over the past few years—questions regarding low energy, little or no sex drive, erectile dysfunction, muscle loss, thinning of hair, and brittle bones. All of these unhealthy symptoms are the more visible signs of hormonal imbalance.

We also receive many questions asking our opinion on hormone replacement therapy. Many times, doctors recommend hormone replacement therapy due to patients' imbalanced hormones—specifically testosterone. Testosterone levels are a good indicator of how the body is aging for both men and women. In response to these questions, we first say that we are not doctors. Next, we start asking some deeper questions: How is your sleep? How would you rate your current stress level? Do you have rest and rejuvenation strategies plugged into your daily routine? Do you consume high-quality omega-3 fats on a daily basis? Do you consume foods high in selenium and zinc? Do you use body-care products that contain parabens? Are you currently exercising and more specifically doing strength training? Do you consume any forms of anti-inflammatories, ibuprofen, or acid blockers on a daily basis? Are you currently taking any prescription medications such as a statin for lowering cholesterol? Many medications can compromise your hormonal balance, and most people are not even aware of the cascade of side effects that may take place by taking some of these medications. Let's begin with the basics: Hormone therapy may be an option down the road, but it is not the place to begin your journey improving your hormonal balance.

Let's try to manage this issue upstream instead of dealing with the waterfall of side effects later on. Chronic stress has a powerful impact on your hormones, especially cortisol and testosterone. Cortisol is a stress hormone and testosterone is a building or sex hormone. If your stress hormones (cortisol) are fired too often, then your building hormones (testosterone) will be compromised, leading to an imbalance of testosterone. This is one reason we try to help people understand that even if they start down the hormone therapy path, it may not be a very effective strategy due to the high levels of

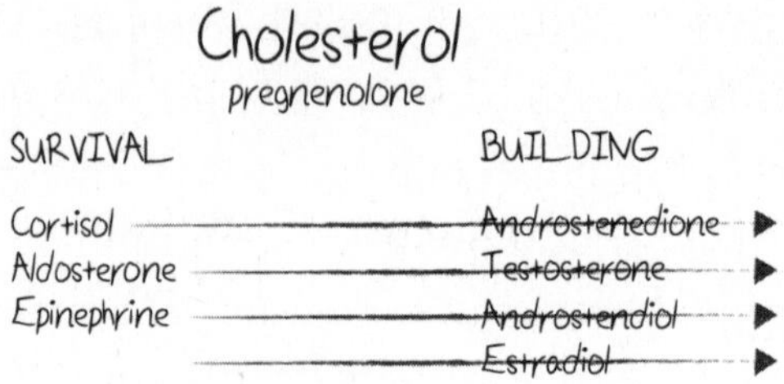

Cholesterol
pregnenolone

SURVIVAL   BUILDING

Cortisol ———————— Androstenedione ▶
Aldosterone ———————— Testosterone ▶
Epinephrine ———————— Androstendiol ▶
                    ———————— Estradiol ▶

FIGURE 8.3   Cortisol Steal.

stress hormones circulating in the bloodstream (Figure 8.3). Integrating rest and rejuvenation strategies into your daily life, along with quality nutrition and daily movement, is the fastest way to get your hormones back into balance. The human body has a powerful ability to heal if given the right resources.

Case Study

A few years ago, I received a phone call from a senior executive of an organization that On Target Living was working with. Greg was an extremely fit and healthy 53-year-old male and was taking no medications, but was concerned that his testosterone level was low.

Greg was a little frustrated and still not completely convinced there was an organic solution to improve his testosterone level. I assured him, from my own personal experience, that Greg could boost his testosterone level by developing a systematic process of how he RESTS, EATS, and MOVES.

We began our training by learning about hormones and getting enough rest. We began discussing his sleep patterns and why getting enough sleep is critical for creating hormonal balance. We then discussed implementing micro and macro breaks into his day, week, and month. We then dove deep into his nutritional habits. It was not what Greg was currently eating that was the problem, it was what he was missing. We added a balance of healthy omega-3 and omega-6 fats, along with foods high in selenium and zinc. We then modified his strength training routine by adding a change in intensity levels each month to stimulate his testosterone. Slowly, step by step, Greg followed the process until these habits turning into daily rituals.

Nine months later I received a phone call from Greg informing me that his blood test came back with 120-point increase in his total testosterone—Greg was extremely happy to share the news with me!

Many months later while Greg was introducing me as a keynote speaker at his National Sales Conference he begins to tell his story. He tells the audience about his low testosterone level, how he met with me, and how he started following the process to improve his testosterone level. But here is the kicker—I never asked Greg his WHY—why was he so concerned about his low testosterone level? I just assumed like many men in their 50s Greg wanted to be his best. While on stage Greg started going deeper and sharing his personal life. Greg told the audience he and his wife were having trouble getting pregnant and Greg thought his low testosterone level could be part of the problem. To the shock of the entire audience, including me, Greg announced that his wife was pregnant with their first child. Today, at age 58, Greg and his wife have two beautiful children. Never underestimate the power of the human body to self-correct when given the right formula.

Here is a snapshot of Greg's new plan to boost his testosterone level:

1. Sleep: increased the amount of sleep by 45–60 minutes each night—targeted eight hours five to six times per week; also decreased the temperature in the bedroom to under 65 degrees and no electronics one hour prior to bed.
2. Diaphragmatic or belly breathing: one- to two-minute breathing breaks, two to three times each day.
3. Epsom salt bath: one to two times per week for 10 minutes.
4. Frozen wheatgrass cubes: four cubes each morning.

5. Spirulina/chlorella: 30–40 tablets spread throughout the day.
6. Cod liver oil: two tablespoons per day.
7. Flaxseeds and hemp seeds: two tablespoons two to four times per week.
8. Pumpkin seeds and Brazil nuts: two tablespoons each day.
9. Breakfast: oatmeal or millet, frozen dark cherries or berries, cacao nibs, variety of nuts, and plant-based milk.
10. Strength training: changed amount of reps each month— month 1, reps of 5 with high load; month 2, reps of 8 with moderate load; month 3, reps of 13 with a lighter load.

After 9 months Greg had increased his testosterone to 498, an increase of 120 points!

Now it's time to learn how to build your *capacity* by plugging sustainable *rest* and *rejuvenation* strategies into your daily routine.

This is our REST methodology (Figure 8.4). These are simple, straightforward strategies and tactics that can be easily implemented

FIGURE 8.4 REST methodology.

throughout your entire organization, building a culture of greater health and performance!

REST Methodology

1. Breathing

One of the most powerful and effective methods to bring more balance, rest, and rejuvenation back into a person's life is to learn how to breathe using the diaphragm, or as many people call it *belly breathing*. You learned in Chapter 5 the calming power of breath awareness for focus as well as how important the diaphragm muscle is to the human body. Your abdominal muscles help move the diaphragm and give more power to empty the lungs; this is one reason maintaining a strong core is essential for more efficient breathing and greater health. There are two types of breathing—chest breathing and diaphragmatic, or belly, breathing. So, what is the big deal about diaphragmatic breathing? Diaphragmatic breathing can decrease the workload on the heart and lungs by over 50 percent, balances the autonomic nervous system, lowers blood pressure, relaxes the mind, improves sleep, and helps keep your pH in balance. If you happen to be a chronic chest breather, you put more stress on your heart and lungs, and you probably have less energy, problems sleeping, and hormonal imbalances.

The science behind diaphragmatic breathing is predicated on balancing the autonomic nervous system. Whenever you take a slow breath using the diaphragm, the vagus nerve that is attached at the base of the diaphragm fires up into the brain signaling the parasympathetic nervous system (brake) to turn on and the sympathetic nervous system (gas) to turn off, giving the mind and body a little relaxation break! Heart rate goes down, blood pressure drops, digestion improves, and energy increases. Your brain waves slow down and emotions become more balanced.

How do you know if you are a chest or a diaphragmatic breather? If you take more than 12 breaths per minute, you are most likely a chest breather. A typical chest breather takes 22,000 or more breaths per day, as compared to a diaphragmatic breather who takes 9,000 to 13,000 breaths per day. It is pretty simple to see how much more efficient diaphragmatic breathing is and how much less stress it places on the entire body. Is it possible to learn how to become a diaphragmatic or belly breather? For sure; in fact it is one of the first strategies we teach at our live events, retreats, and coaching sessions.

Here are five easy tips to help you begin the practice of diaphragmatic or belly breathing:

1. Lie on a flat surface, foam roller, or bed. Bend your knees or place a pillow under your knees. Put one hand on your belly and the other hand on your chest, and close your eyes and mouth.
2. Breathe in slowly through the nose so that your belly moves out against your hand. Your chest should not be moving. As you take a deep breath, your belly expands out, and as you exhale your belly will come back in.
3. Feel the coolness of the breath through the nose (breath awareness). By focusing on your breath, your mind will begin to clear and your entire body will begin to relax!
4. Practice this exercise every day for one to five minutes.
5. If you want to practice diaphragmatic breathing while standing or sitting, follow the same principles and maintain good posture.

Diaphragmatic breathing and breath awareness is your first step in learning how to control your mind. Performing diaphragmatic breathing can be extremely therapeutic and with regular practice can become your standard way of breathing and on-demand stress reduction.

2. Sleep

One of the most powerful ways to improve your health and enhance performance is to get a good night's sleep. What is sleep exactly? Sleep is a natural state of rest for the mind and body. Being awake is catabolic (breaks you down) and sleep is anabolic (builds you up). Sleep boosts your immune system, balances hormones, builds up energy, and bolsters brain health. How many times have you walked into work with your eyes glued shut and barely functioning because you didn't get a good night's sleep? Having an occasional night when we do not sleep well is very common, especially as we age. Very rarely do you hear about sleep problems with our kids! The heavier demands of adult life always find a way to throw a wrench in our sleep cycle.

Getting quality sleep has become a major health problem around the world today. Lack of sleep destroys the mind and body. Poor sleep can lead to many health-related problems such as heart disease, hormonal imbalances, obesity, headaches, high blood pressure, dementia, Alzheimer's, poor digestion, imbalanced pH, joint pain, and chronic inflammation. Lack of sleep ages the human body very quickly. One of the fastest growing groups of medications today is for sleep. The answer to getting a better night's sleep does not come in a pill bottle!

So how do we begin our journey toward getting a better night's sleep? Did you know that before the invention of the electric light bulb in 1879 most people were averaging over 10 hours of sleep per night? Today that number has dropped under six hours per night! Is it possible to improve the quality and quantity of your sleep? Let's begin by learning more about normal sleep as this may help you recognize what you may be missing in your quest for a better night's sleep.

For an activity that we all participate in every 24 hours, most of us know very little about sleep. There are four stages of sleep that we cycle through every 90–120 minutes (Figure 8.5). Stages 1–2 prepare the body for deep sleep, which happens in Stage 3. During

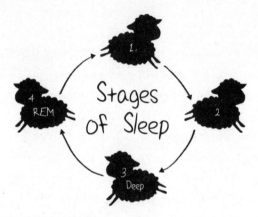

FIGURE 8.5 Stages of sleep.

Stage 3, the human body goes into full repair mode—hormones such as testosterone, estrogen, and growth hormone are all busy repairing the damage done by the rigors of the day. Stage 4 is REM sleep (rapid eye movement). In this stage the brain is healing itself. REM sleep is when we dream; as the night goes on we get into REM sleep more quickly. This is one reason why it is so important to get 7.5 to 8.5 hours of sleep—so you get enough REM sleep. If you are sleeping 4 to 5 hours per night, you get very little REM sleep. By simply sleeping 8 hours per night, you may double the amount of REM sleep (Figure 8.6)!

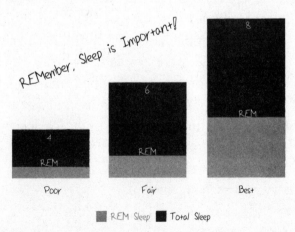

FIGURE 8.6 REM sleep graph.

Why has getting a good night's sleep become such a challenge? Greater daily demands creating higher levels of stress can lead to various forms of insomnia. Too much alcohol, energy drinks, caffeine, processed foods, and certain prescription medications all may negatively affect the quality of our sleep.

How to Sleep Better

Step 1: Value sleep. Step 1 sounds simple, but do you truly recognize how important getting enough sleep is in your overall health and performance? Respecting the value of sleep is Step 1! Sleep is one of the best investments to make in yourself.

Step 2: Establish and maintain a circadian rhythm. Keeping a regular sleep schedule is critical in maintaining a synchronized circadian rhythm or cycle—conditioning the mind and body to expect specific sleep and wake-up times. Try to consistently go to bed and wake up at the same times, even if they aren't ideal at first. Also, try to add an additional 30 minutes to your sleep schedule!

Step 3: Get sunlight. Absorbing natural sunlight a few times per day helps stimulate the pineal gland to regulate the production of your sleep hormone, melatonin. During the day melatonin is low, but as nighttime approaches and darkness sets in, melatonin levels rise. As melatonin levels increase, drowsiness sets in. If you are inside all day long, your pineal gland may have a difficult time recognizing day or night, leading to an imbalance of melatonin production. Getting 20–30 minutes of sunlight, especially in the morning or early afternoon, has a powerful impact on melatonin production. Also, a healthy gut releases a good amount of melatonin, which we address at length in Chapter 9.

Stress is also a killer for melatonin production. As cortisol levels increase, melatonin levels decrease. Another reason why having rest and rejuvenation strategies is essential for optimal health is that performance and getting a better night's sleep are not mutually exclusive; you can't have one without the other!

Step 4: Set up your sleep environment. One of the keys for getting a good night's sleep at home or on the road is creating a great sleep environment.

- ○ Darkness—make your environment dark. Light kills melatonin! This includes various electronic media—blue light emitted abundantly in our daily lives from TV, laptops, and smartphones. All of these light sources increase cortisol levels and disrupt circadian rhythms, which leads to poor sleep.
- ○ Quiet—keep your environment quiet. Some relaxing sound or white noise can also be helpful in drowning out noise.
- ○ Cool—keep your sleep environment cool. Keeping the temperature at 60–65 degrees plays a huge role stimulating the parasympathetic nervous system, making the body slow down and relax.

Step 5: Have a caffeine curfew. Don't drink or eat caffeine after 2:00 p.m.

Step 6: Engage in diaphragmatic breathing and breath awareness. Diaphragmatic breathing coupled with breath awareness relaxes the mind and body.

Step 7: Increase mineral intake. Magnesium is the mineral of relaxation. It can help with headaches, blood pressure, atrial fibrillation, and staying asleep. Green foods such as wheatgrass, spirulina/chlorella, kale, spinach, and leafy greens are extremely high in magnesium. Cacao nibs, coconut, oatmeal, chia and flaxseeds, white figs, raisins, and an Epsom salt bath (absorbed through the skin) prior to bed are all great ways to get more magnesium into your body.

Step 8: Move daily. Daily movement has a way of burning up the stress hormones, allowing a calming effect post-exercise. Move your body daily to improve the quality of your sleep!

3. White Space

Building white space—planned recovery—into your day is essential for optimal health, increased capacity, and greater performance. Here are a few white space activities you can plug into your life:

- Massage
- 24-hour vacation
- Day at the spa
- Electronic break
- Cold shower
- Epsom salt bath
- Classical music
- Belly breathing
- Movies

4. Meditation

Having you ever had some amazing insights while taking a shower, driving down the highway, or going on a long walk? What is it that allowed your mind to open up? Most likely it was because your mind was relaxed and free and was able to search for the answer and solution you needed. This is the benefit of meditation. Meditation allows you to quiet the mind. Meditation is a conscious relaxation exercise, with the goal of clearing the mind, creating peace and serenity, and opening yourself to greater insights. Start your meditation journey by paying attention to your breath. Find a quiet place, sit upright with good posture and hands resting on your thighs, close your eyes and mouth, and focus on your breath.

Three Levels of Deep Relaxation

1. Structural or muscular—tension-release exercises, imagery techniques, massage
2. Autonomic—regulation of the lungs, 2:1 breathing technique, diaphragmatic breathing
3. Concentration—meditation (internal), gazing (external)

Deep Relaxation Leads to the Following

- Reduced stress and tension at work
- Increased balance and flexibility
- Strengthened immune system
- Flexible mind for creative problem solving
- Heighten sense of awareness
- Intuition and perceive others more clearly

5. Stretch/Foam Roller

Plug into your day a 30- to 60-second stretch break multiple times each day. The standing wall extension, standing upward and downward dog, and half-moon against the wall are three easy stretches that cover lots of ground in a short amount of time. (Chapter 10 will show these exercises.)

Also, using a foam roller for one to two minutes each day can improve your posture, decrease muscle tension, and help you feel rejuvenated. Try it whenever you need a little extra boost to get through the day!

6. Nature

Take a walk in nature. Look and listen to all the beauty around you. Stare at the moon or clouds. Start to understand your place in the grand scheme of things and put your life into perspective. Despite the fact that all of our lives are consumed with endless distractions that create more stress and anxiety, the endless universe continues to hum along with magnificent efficiency. Once we start viewing ourselves as mere blips on the cosmic radar, instead of having everything in our material world orbit around us, the weight we carry on our shoulders begins to lessen. Nature allows you to get lost in the moment and just be.

Take the time to build more rest and rejuvenation into your daily life. Pick one area you would like to improve upon from the preceding strategies and commit yourself to it. We all need to recharge our proverbial batteries to bring our best selves into the next day. We need to clear the cache and push the reset button on stress. Don't underestimate the power of rest and recovery for supercharging your organization!

Key Point

We all will have stress. Most of it we can control with our thoughts, but even so, the real solution to stress is to implement more thoughtful rest on a weekly, daily, or hourly basis.

9

EAT

You are what you eat is not a cliché—it's one of life's most fundamental truths. So why aren't more organizations trying to understand nutrition and how it impacts performance? An organization is fueled by people and we are all powered by what we eat, so let's start supercharging the workforce with rocket fuel instead of regular unleaded!

Chris's Story

For over 17 years I worked at one of the largest hospital-based health clubs in the United States. I had the privilege of working with some of the best and brightest professionals in the health-care space. Toward the end of my time working in the health system, I was asked to attend a weeklong training with over 300 directors to develop strategies to improve performance throughout the entire hospital system. It was quite a spectacle. Each morning we started the day with a large selection of doughnuts, fruit, coffee, and soda pop. For lunch, it was a croissant sandwich with turkey, beef, or tuna, lettuce, tomato, and cheese; chips; apple; cookie; and soda pop, and if you wanted water you could use a cup at the drinking fountain. They made sure to save the best for last—at the afternoon break, we had the largest cookies you have ever seen, along with more soda pop. In no time, a room full of 300 top performers were paralyzed by a total food coma!

Each day I brought in my own cooler full of whole foods and water. This included my breakfast of oatmeal on the run, my lunch of a big salad full of vegetables and chicken, and snacks of fresh fruit and nuts. The first day people were making comments about my cooler full of food: "Hey, isn't that the health guy from the club!" But by day two people were asking multiple questions about my intake: "What are you eating? How did you put it together? Where did I buy it? Why did I feel compelled to bring my own food?" I almost wanted to set up a booth outside the conference room and host a mini-seminar just to satisfy their curiosity! I helped them understand how important a little nutrition planning was in controlling my energy, focus, and performance.

After leaving my career in the health system, I witnessed the same self-defeating mentality in corporate America. Rarely did you see healthy, high-performance foods and beverages at conferences or during meetings. Organizations bring in their most talented people to learn and grow only to fuel their teams with junk foods and sugary beverages. How do you expect your organization to grow and perform on low-octane fuel?

Nutrition 101

Let's begin with a better understanding of nutrition. Think of nutrition as the process of being nourished. When we eat or drink, the body breaks down the nutrients to fuel, grow, and repair itself. Nutrition starts with the quality of food and beverages you ingest. Next, how does the body break down these nutrients and absorb them into the body? It is what we ingest and assimilate that fuels the body. This process is called digestion and underscores the critical factor for optimal health and human performance—it's not what we eat, but how we absorb and assimilate the nutrients. During digestion, the entire body is working not only to break down what you consume, but also to help these nutrients be absorbed into the body. After digestion, the body moves into the elimination phase. Elimination is the process of excreting what is not needed during the digestive process. So, what happens if the body is not using the foods or beverages that were ingested or not eliminated? These foods or beverages become stored, leading to toxicity—and this is where many of our problems begin!

Upwards of 75 percent of our immune system is based on the health of the gut. If your gut is not healthy, you are not healthy. We have seen an explosion of digestive health problems in the past 20 years:

- Acid reflux
- IBS
- Constipation
- Diarrhea
- Gluten intolerance
- Food allergies
- Kidney stones
- Gout

Did you know that approximately 50–75 percent of your production of serotonin, the neurotransmitter that triggers happiness and helps build melatonin, comes from the gut? A healthy gut is imperative for greater health along with getting a better night's sleep. Treating many of these problems with medications in most cases is not fixing the problem—it only controls the symptoms.

Having a healthy digestive system is critical for your health and success. Here are a few tips to improve your digestion and gut health:

- *Cut out the processed foods and beverages.* Your body craves whole foods that are loaded with valuable nutrients. The more processed a food is, the less nutrients it contains.

- *Chew your food.* Save your gut a little extra work by breaking down the raw material in your mouth first.
- *Eat more live foods.* The fresher and more natural a food source is, the more enzymes, good bacteria, and phyto-nutrients it contains to aid digestion.
- *Balance your pH.* Your body must be in a more balanced alkaline state to digest properly.
- *Bring on the friendly bacteria.* Live foods, raw sauerkraut, coconut, kefir or yogurt, frozen wheatgrass cubes, spirulina/chlorella, most greens, ginger, kombucha, apple cider vinegar with a little local honey, and water are great ways to improve your gut health.
- *Use only high-quality body care products.* Ensure your cosmetic products don't contain parabens, phthalates, synthetic colors, or triclosan.

Now that you have a little better understanding of nutrition and digestion, let's cover the three On Target Living principles to better illustrate the science behind the methodology.

On Target Living Principles

Gravity is consistent and reliable in its results. If you step off a building, you're going to fall. The lack of consistency in the health and performance space has led to confusion. With new trends every week, it is difficult to break through the clutter. Our solution is to follow these three On Target Living Principles: cellular health, pH balance, and the source. These three principles are the bedrock of On Target Living, and they will never change.

1. Cellular Health

Our first principle is cellular health. Your energy, your waistline, your health, and your overall performance all begin at the cellular level (Figure 9.1). The human body has over 50 trillion cells— now that is a lot of cells! One of the most beautiful aspects of the human body is its ability to adapt and heal itself. Each day the cells of the human body are going through constant change. In fact, the human body turns over millions per day. Begin your focus on getting healthy at the cellular level. As you begin to feed your cells high-quality nutrients, your skin and hair begin to look better, digestion improves, energy improves, clothes fit differently, inflammation begins to disappear, cholesterol profile gets back in balance, and blood glucose improves. Your cells are slowly transforming and the body is getter healthier!

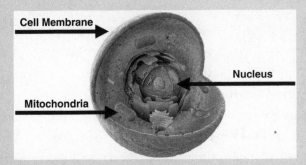

FIGURE 9.1 Human cell.

2. pH Balance

Our second principle is pH balance (Figure 9.2). Growing up, I (Chris) had unhealthy skin for almost 15 years of my life, which included psoriasis, dandruff, and terrible acne; I was prescribed oral medications and topical creams, but nothing seemed to work. My doctors kept telling my parents I just had sensitive

(Continued)

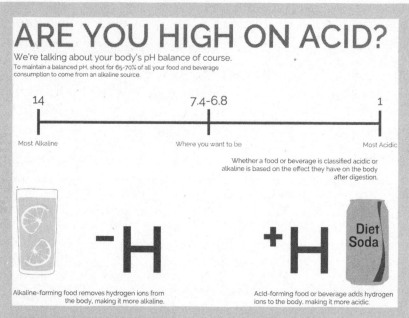

ARE YOU HIGH ON ACID?

We're talking about your body's pH balance of course.

To maintain a balanced pH, shoot for 65-70% of all your food and beverage consumption to come from an alkaline source.

14	7.4-6.8	1
Most Alkaline	Where you want to be	Most Acidic

Whether a food or beverage is classified acidic or alkaline is based on the effect they have on the body after digestion.

-H

+H Diet Soda

Alkaline-forming food removes hydrogen ions from the body, making it more alkaline.

Acid-forming food or beverage adds hydrogen ions to the body, making it more acidic.

FIGURE 9.2 pH balance.

skin. I did not have sensitive skin—I was poor eater! It was not until I changed what I was eating and drinking that my skin began to improve. Never once did anyone, including my doctors, mention anything about pH balance or anything about what I was eating and drinking. Every food and beverage has an acid or alkaline characteristic and is measured on a pH scale of 1–14, with 1 being the most acidic and 14 the most alkaline. Some foods and beverages are more acid forming and some are alkaline forming. Ideally, the human blood pH should be slightly alkaline, between 7.35 and 7.45. Thank goodness, the human body has checks and balances to keep our pH in balance, or we would all die quickly! But if your body has to work overtime to maintain a balanced pH, this is where the trouble begins. Many health problems can be linked to an acid-forming diet and high levels of stress. Consuming too much coffee, caffeine, soda pop, energy drinks, alcohol, protein, processed foods, sweetened beverages, artificial sweeteners, and medications combined with high levels of stress can all lead to an imbalanced pH. To improve your pH balance, *eat* closer to the center of the food target (see Figure 9.5 on page 148), get adequate *rest*, and *move* your body daily.

3. Source

Understanding our third principle, the *source*, will help you cut through all the noise of information and allow you to make better nutritional decisions. When you encounter a food, beverage, or supplement and want to know if it is healthy or unhealthy, always begin by asking the question, What's the *source*? If you focus on eating foods and drinking beverages as close to their natural source as possible, you will be practicing the *source* principle.

Here are few *source* foods that may have been given a bad rap. Is a banana good for you? Yes! Bananas are high in potassium and magnesium, reduce heat in the body, and act as a pre-biotic for a healthy gut; plus, they are perfectly wrapped and taste great!

Is coconut healthy? We are not talking about the processed coconut found in many candy bars or Grandma's German chocolate cake recipe, but real coconut. Coconut is a healthy saturated fat that is high in magnesium and potassium, and is rich in lauric and caprylic acids, which are loaded with antiviral and antifungal properties, making coconut extremely beneficial for digestion, heart, skin, and brain health.

If you are looking for the most nutritious, most absorbable, inexpensive, least-processed foods, then the closer you are to the *source* the better (Figure 9.3).

(Continued)

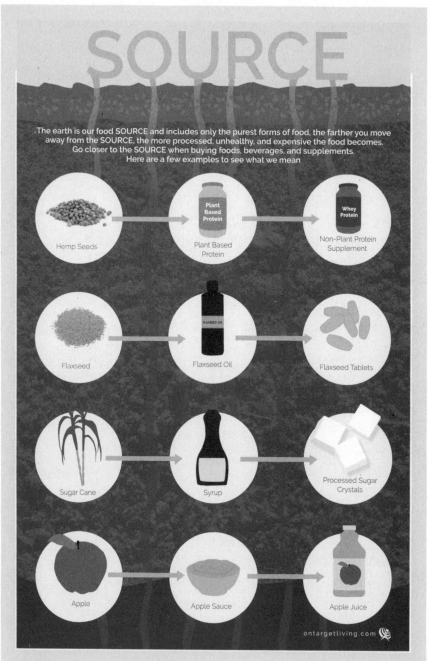

FIGURE 9.3 The source.

FIGURE 9.4 *EAT* methodology.

Now that you have a better understanding of nutrition, let's get cracking on the fun part—the *how*. Following the *EAT* methodology (Figure 9.4) can take the mystery out of eating healthy and will help you build a solid nutritional foundation that can easily be instilled throughout your entire organization. Start slowly and continue to upgrade your nutritional habits!

EAT Methodology

Step 1: Hydration

Water is essential for life and keeping the body healthy. Did you know that the human body is 70–75 percent water? That the human brain is made up predominantly of water and fat? Water is the universal solvent for every organism and the superconductor for better health.

Water

Water is the body's cleansing and waste-removal fluid. Water carries nutrients and oxygen—90 percent of your blood is composed of water for that very reason. Water also aids in digestion and metabolism. If you want to have greater focus, energy, and health, and expanded capacity, drinking high-quality water is an excellent first step. Here is what you need to know about water and fueling better performance.

How Much Should I Drink? How much water is optimal per day? Ideally, consume half your body weight in ounces each day. For example, if you weigh 200 pounds, then try to consume 100 ounces each day. If you are currently drinking only 30 ounces of water per day, try to take it up to 50 ounces per day—the key is to drink more water throughout your day. One of the healthiest habits you can start tomorrow is drinking 10 ounces of water first thing each and every morning. Also, we recommend having water on your bed stand at night so you can have a sip or two if you wake up during the night. Staying well hydrated is critical to your overall health and performance.

Water Quality As you increase the quantity of drinking water, start upgrading the quality to enhance your energy and focus!

- Tap water—If you drink tap water as your primary water source, we recommend using some type of filtration system. Tap water can have high levels of chlorine and other toxic ingredients.
- Bottled water—When purchasing bottled water, look for spring or artesian water over purified or distilled.
- Mineral water—One of the easiest ways to improve your health is to drink mineral water a few times per week. Choose only mineral water with natural occurring carbonation. You

can also purchase mineral water without carbonation. Add a slice of lemon, lime, or orange, or add a shot of juice for a healthy flavor boost.

- Ionized filtration system—If you want a great water source in the convenience of your home, we highly recommend an ionized filtration system.

Beverages of Choice

Here are a few of the most popular beverage types. You don't have to deny yourself completely—just try to upgrade whenever possible.

- Coffee—Whenever possible buy organic coffee. Coffee and tea are two crops with high pesticide levels. Also, if you use a coffee creamer avoid creamers with trans fats and get a creamer closer to the *source*.
- Tea—We are big fans of herbal teas like peppermint, ginger, and licorice root. Ginger happens to be my favorite. We like the taste and the smell, and it's great for gut health and digestion. Ginger root can be found in the grocery store, shave, peel, and add to hot water. When choosing your favorite tea, buy organic whenever possible.
- Plant-based milk—We are not a fan of cow's milk due to the body's inability to digest it completely. Unless you have a cow outside your door, we recommend moving to plant-based milks such as coconut, almond, cashew, or hemp milk. Plant-based milks can also be made easily right in your own kitchen.
- Smoothies—Adding a healthy and delicious smoothie recipe to your nutritional routine can be easy. Our favorite smoothie recipe—chocolate chip mint—consists of coconut flakes, hemp seeds, Brazil nuts, dates, mint leaves, spinach, coconut water, and cacao nibs. Just blend for 30–45 seconds for a delicious and nutritious midday energy boost!

- Juicing—Juicing is an easy way to introduce high-quality nutrients in your diet without sacrificing flavor! It is as simple as buying a juice extractor and experimenting with your favorite fruits and vegetables! Our favorite juice recipe consists of celery, apples, carrots, and beets. We make enough for a few days and store it in the refrigerator in a glass container. We also buy organic dark cherry juice, pomegranate, or cranberry juice to use with my ground flax or to flavor our water a bit.

Step 2: Superfoods

It can be challenging to know what foods, supplements, or herbs someone should use in their quest for greater health, energy, and vitality. We find many people want to target a specific need or problem with a specific food, supplement, or herb. Want to decrease the risk of catching a cold? Take vitamin C. Want to improve digestion? Take a probiotic. Want to lower cholesterol? Take niacin. Want to decrease inflammation? Take an aspirin or ibuprofen. We have to get away from the mindset of taking foods, supplements, herbs, or medications for isolated needs. The human body is not designed to heal this way!

Imagine a food—not a drug and not a typical food that gives you a few vitamins, minerals and energy, but a potent superfood—powerful enough to improve your cholesterol profile, lower your blood pressure, and significantly decrease your risk of heart disease, cancer, and type 2 diabetes. Superfoods are nature's perfect delivery system for maximum health and human performance.

What Is a Superfood?

Superfoods are nutrient-dense whole foods that offer many amazing health benefits packed into a small amount of food. Many people think they eat pretty healthy foods, and this may be true in many cases, but are they only just filling in one piece of the puzzle?

Finding the highest quality nutrients can be very challenging and confusing. That's the beauty of superfoods—they fuel a holistic nutrition profile instead of just a few. What we find is that most people are missing high-quality forms of chlorophyll, minerals, and omega-3 and omega-6 fats. Adding a few superfoods to your nutritional plan is a simple and efficient way to build your nutrition plan without worrying if you are getting the basic nutrients your body needs! Once the foundational basics are in place, then specific foods, spices, or herbs may be added to amplify individual needs. There are so many superfoods to choose from! In fact, just about every brightly colored vegetable or fruit, along with most nuts, seeds, beans, herbs, and spices, could be classified as superfoods. Here are our top superfoods:

1. *Wheatgrass*. Wheatgrass is the highest raw source of minerals in the world, with over 90 minerals, making it extremely alkaline. Wheatgrass is also supercharged with chlorophyll. Together, this powerful combination strengthens our cells, cleanses the body, aids digestion, improves metabolism, and enhances your skin, hair, and nails. You want to consume unpasteurized outdoor wheatgrass that is flash frozen. Melt two to five wheatgrass ice cubes in a glass of water and drink first thing in the morning on an empty stomach for greatest absorption.

2. *Spirulina/chlorella*. These two freshwater algae are super high in chlorophyll and help build the immune system, detoxify the body, and improve digestion. Spirulina/chlorella are also high in protein, which makes them an ideal choice for any vegan or vegetarian diet. Spirulina/chlorella are inexpensive and easy to take—just swallow the tablets with water. Begin with 10–15 tablets per day and slowly build up to 20–30 tablets per day. Spirulina/chlorella aids in digestion and are best taken prior to eating a meal.

3. *Cod liver oil.* This omega-3 fat contains EPA and DHA, which contribute to a healthy heart and brain, hormonal balance, and decreased inflammation. Cod liver oil also helps to improve cellular function, energy, and mood, and aids in weight control. Cod liver oil also has a higher level of vitamin D content. Don't be afraid of the taste—this is not your grandma's cod liver oil! Recommended adult dosage, one to two tablespoons per day (1,500–3,000 mg of EPA/DHA per day).

4. *Flaxseeds/chia seeds/hemp seeds.* Flaxseeds and chia seeds are very high in omega-3s (ALA) and contain antiviral, antifungal, antibacterial, and anticancer properties. Hemp seeds are high in healthy omega-6s (LA and GLA), along with high levels of fiber and protein. These super omegas help to lower inflammation, balance hormones, and improve digestion. Flaxseeds must be ground to reap their wonderful benefits. The recommended serving is one to two tablespoons per day and it can easily be added to your favorite smoothie, cereal, yogurt, or salad, or with one to two ounces of juice. We actually use these superseeds as our protein powder replacement!

5. *Coconut.* Coconut is a healthy saturated fat high in lauric, capric, and caprylic acids. These acids have antifungal and antiviral properties that contribute to healthy digestion, skin, and hair. Coconut also contains medium chain triglycerides great for improved metabolism and brain health. Aim for one tablespoon of extra virgin coconut oil or organic coconut flakes per day.

6. *Cacao nibs or cacao powder.* Cacao is the raw unprocessed form of chocolate and is high in magnesium, manganese, zinc and iron. These vitamins and minerals are essential to enhanced brain and heart health, healthy metabolism, and enhancing relaxation and recovery due to high levels of magnesium. Aim for one tablespoon per day. Mix in oatmeal, smoothies, or in your favorite trail mix blend.

Start slowly. Pick just one or two of these superfoods to start mixing into your daily diet. You will be shocked at just how quickly your performance improves by supplementing and upgrading your diet with these powerful superfoods!

Sample: Superfood Starter Plan

1. Cod liver oil: one to two tablespoons/day
2. Spirulina/chlorella: 10–30 tablets/day

Big Four Superfoods

1. Frozen wheatgrass ice cubes: two to five/day
2. Cod liver oil: one to two tablespoons/day
3. Spirulina/chlorella: 10–15 tablets/day
4. Flaxseeds or chia seeds: two tablespoons/day

We understand that everyone is in a different spot in regards to their nutrition plan. We are also mindful of how much conflicting and bad information there is on the healthiest foods to eat. Recently there was an article that made our community question a staple superfood we have been recommending for years. The American Heart Association published an article about the harmful effects of coconut oil and saturated fats. One key to understand is that there is always another side to every coin. This article failed to discuss a simple principle that holds true to the test of time: What is the *source*? Any food that is far removed from the original source is likely to be absorbed and digested dramatically differently than one closer to its natural form. Virgin coconut oil is one of nature's most magical foods. We know how many benefits you will get from consuming this superfood in your daily routine; just make sure it's the real deal!

We also wanted to give you an idea of what a typical day looks like for both of us. This routine has taken a long time to establish, and we don't expect you to get here overnight. Chris grew up eating beefaroni and bologna sandwiches with Kool-Aid and Pepsi as his drinks of choice. Matt had a point in college where he didn't eat breakfast and ate an entire package of Oreo cookies at one sitting. We have both come a very long way from those nutritional low points! In our pursuit to feel and perform our best, we looked to establish the best patterns.

Sample of Chris's and Matt's Superfood Day

Chris

6:30 A.M. Water with lemon (10 ounces)

6:35 A.M. Frozen wheatgrass ice cubes (five cubes)

6:40 A.M. Cod liver oil (two tablespoons)

7 A.M. Oatmeal, millet, or teff; frozen dark cherries or blueberries; raisins; cacao powder; macadamia nuts or pecans; cinnamon; cashew or coconut milk

10 A.M. Spirulina/chlorella (20 tablets), apple, Brazil nuts (five)

12:30 P.M. Big salad with vegetables, tongal tuna or chicken, hemp seeds (two tablespoons), raw sauerkraut, avocado, extra virgin olive oil, balsamic vinegar

3:30 P.M. White figs (two), almonds (six), spirulina/chlorella (20 tablets)

7:00 P.M. Organic chicken breast or wild Alaskan Salmon, sweet potato with coconut oil, grilled asparagus

8:00 P.M. Ginger, water, and lemon shot or ground flaxseeds or chia seeds in pomegranate juice (one to two ounces)

Matt

6:45 A.M. Frozen wheatgrass ice cubes (three to four)

6:45 A.M. Cod liver oil (one tablespoon)

8:00 A.M. Oatmeal on the run, teff with cacao and honey, or eggs and veggies and sprouted toast with coconut oil

9:30 A.M. Spirulina/chlorella (20 tablets); banana, orange, nectarine, cherries, or apple

Noon Leftovers or salad with chicken, veggies, and white balsamic vinaigrette

3:00 P.M. Organic food bar, sprouted almonds with dried fruit, dried mango

6:00 P.M. Bison burgers with sweet potato fries or stir-fry with organic brown rice and bok choy

7:30 P.M. Cherry juice with ground flaxseeds or chia seeds (one tablespoon)

8:00 P.M. Fresh pineapple or sliced mango

Step 3: Upgrade Your Macronutrients

Many people ask, "What should I eat to improve my health, energy and expand my capacity?" We tell them to focus on eating the three macronutrients—carbohydrates, proteins, and fats. Macronutrients are the fuel source for our minds and bodies.

- Carbohydrates—*fuel*
- Proteins—*build*
- Fats—*heal*

To help you or your organization learn more about the three macronutrients, along with eating in greater balance and improving food quality, we developed a simple, easy-to-use guide: the Food Target (Figure 9.5). The Food Target focuses on a balance of carbohydrates, proteins, and fats while incorporating and assessing the holistic quality of these nutrients. The Food Target has the lowest nutritional value foods on the outside of the target (poor area) with the most nutritional and most beneficial foods closer to the center of the Food Target (best area). The idea behind the On Target Living lifestyle is to achieve balanced eating around the target while aiming your diet as close to the center of the target as

FIGURE 9.5 The Food Target

NOTE: For the full colored version visit: ontargetliving.com/foodtarget

possible. You will find foods in their most natural state (*source*) closer to the center of the target. Most importantly, the Food Target allows you to change at your desired pace. You don't have to go from the outer ring to the center all at once. The Food Target is meant to be just as forgiving as it is fruitful.

Carbohydrates—Fuel Your Body and Mind!

What is a carbohydrate? Carbohydrates are *sugars*. Carbohydrates are simply sugar chains linked together. The shorter the sugar chain, the more processed or refined the carbohydrate. Conversely a longer chain has more nutritional value. A question we receive at many of our live events is "Is sugar bad?" Our response: It depends on the source of the sugar. Is the sugar you refer to the processed white version or that which occurs in its most natural state like a piece of fruit, sweet potato, or in a fibrous stalk of sugar cane? Imagine if we drove people to the vast sugar cane fields of South Florida and handed them a machete to hack it all down. Most would probably pass out after a few short minutes of exhausting work and wonder why they subjected themselves to this torture in the first place! Sugar cane is hard to cut, extremely fibrous, and difficult to eat. Did you know that sugar cane is also high in minerals and fiber and is a powerful preservative that also happens to be extremely sweet? Once we started processing out all the fiber and minerals for the sake of easier consumption, we started to sacrifice sugar cane's inherent health benefits.

Don't Be Afraid of the Big Bad Wolf!

Over the year's carbohydrates have been getting a bad rap, with most carbohydrates lumped together in one overarching nutrient category. This is a problem; lumping all carbohydrates together is like comparing any consumer product—there are higher and lower quality products. It's necessary to learn how to distinguish between the quality carbohydrates that come from the source and the processed unhealthy carbohydrates that don't. We want to make it clear that high-quality carbohydrates are essential for greater energy, balancing pH, and better health and human performance.

Did you know that your brain needs approximately 400 calories of carbohydrates per day to function properly? Carbohydrate deprivation should not be a fear-based reaction to all the noise and misinformation you're bombarded by.

Carbohydrates also provide the body with valuable fiber, vitamins, minerals, phytochemicals, and antioxidants for the immune and nervous systems. Every fruit, vegetable, whole grain, starch, and legume is a carbohydrate. Your goal each day is to consume approximately 50 percent of your calories from quality carbohydrates. Examples of quality carbohydrates include apples, oranges, bananas, figs, berries, leafy greens, asparagus, beets, broccoli, rolled oats, millet, sweet or red potatoes, and lentils. These optimal carbohydrates strengthen your mind and body and fuel better performance. What's led us astray is the overconsumption of the unhealthy, processed carbohydrates like cereals, white bread, chips/crackers, instant potatoes, and soda pop, just to name a few. These refined carbohydrates have been processed and stripped of essential nutrients and are lacking the essential fiber, vitamins, minerals, phytochemicals, and antioxidants we need. When someone says, "I am on a low-carbohydrate diet," what does that actually mean? Are you also not eating vegetables, fruits, ancient grains, starches, or legumes?

Removing a macronutrient will eventually create a macro problem.

Proteins—Build Your Body!

Proteins are the building blocks of life. Protein plays a vital role in every cell of the body. Proteins create hormones, maintain the immune system, build muscle, transport vitamins, and maintain our blood, skin, and connective tissue. So, what is a protein exactly? Proteins are simply amino acids. More importantly, the body can't manufacture essential amino acids, so we must ingest them in order to grow and repair ourselves. Similar to the earlier discussion on carbohydrates, people can't stop asking questions about them: "How do I get more protein in my diet?" Many people believe that the more protein you consume, the more you will be a lean, mean, health-conscious machine! Do you ever hear someone say, "I want to add more carbohydrates to my smoothie?" More and more marketing is selling the idea that higher protein, with little or no carbs, is the one true way to achieve health and human performance. Drinks, bars, and smoothies are now advertising 30-plus grams of protein with only one gram of carbohydrate!

Having enough high-quality proteins in your diet is essential for optimal health and greater performance in all aspects of your life. But just like our discussion about carbohydrates, the real focus should begin with quality proteins—not overloading on them. Just like carbohydrates, not all proteins are created equal! High-quality protein sources may include organic meats such as chicken, turkey, bison, grass-fed beef, and game meats; eggs; wild-caught fish; vegetables; oats; millet; teff; spirulina/chlorella; hemp seeds; pumpkins seeds; Brazil nuts; macadamia nuts; almonds; and walnuts. Use the Food Target to help guide your protein choices. Your goal each day is to consume approximately 25 percent of your daily calories from high-quality protein sources!

Fats—Heal Your Body

One of the fastest and easiest ways to improve your overall health is to blend a variety of healthy fats into your diet. Despite what you grew up hearing, healthy fats will actually lower blood pressure and balance cholesterol levels. Bottom line—healthy fats heal the body! Back in the 1980s the nutritional craze was all about low or no fat. The mentality was predicated on the premise that fats alone made people fat and led to higher levels of heart disease due to clogged arteries. Thank goodness, this myth did not last more than a decade. Today the science is crystal clear: healthy fats are essential for optimal health. If you have unbalanced hormones you are most likely not getting enough rest and not consuming enough high-quality omega-3 and omega-6 fats. If you are experiencing type 2 diabetes, one of the best things you can do is restore cellular health, which begins by consuming healthy fats. Do you want a healthy and high-performing brain? Then it is a must to consume healthy fats such as coconut oil and cod liver oil.

Types of Healthy Fats There are four categories of healthy fats: saturated, monounsaturated, omega-3, and omega-6s:

1. Saturated fats—organic coconut flakes, extra virgin coconut oil, most nuts and seeds.
2. Monounsaturated fats—almonds, almond butter, avocados, macadamia nuts, cashews, pecans, hazelnuts, and extra virgin olive oil.
3. Omega-3 essential fatty acids—cod liver oil, flaxseeds, chia seeds, walnuts, salmon, trout, and sardines.
4. Omega-6 essential fatty acids—hemp seeds, Brazil nuts, pumpkin seeds, sunflower seeds, evening primrose oil, and black current seed oil.

Use the Food Target to help guide your fat choices. Your goal each day is to consume approximately 25 percent of your calories from high-quality fats.

Step 4: Meal Patterning

After you begin to upgrade the quality of what you are eating and drinking, it is then time to focus on the frequency of meals or meal patterning. One of the first things people do when trying to lose weight is to cut calories by skipping meals. Skipping meals actually slows down your metabolism and alerts the body to release more of the fat-storing enzyme, lipoprotein lipase. Lipoprotein lipase becomes more sensitive when meals are skipped; it's one of the body's safety mechanisms to protect against starvation. Did you know that one of the key strategies for sumo wrestlers to gain weight is to eat one extremely large meal per day?

If your goal is to increase metabolism and create more sustainable energy throughout the day, then start controlling portion sizes and create a feeling of being satisfied. Spread your calories throughout the day by eating every three to four hours.

Cleansing the Bathtub

A fantastic method for improving your metabolism, digestion, and overall health, is to fast multiple times per week for at least 12 hours. If you had your last meal at 7:00 P.M. then you would not eat again until 7:00 A.M. the next morning. Many people struggle with digestive health concerns. Allowing your gut to rest for at least 12 hours can make all the difference. Think of your body as a bathtub—you have to drain the tub; by fasting for 12 hours, it allows the body enough time to clean, eliminate, and repair the trillions of cells necessary for optimal health. Once your 12 hours is up, resume eating every three to four hours. By eating frequent, small meals, you naturally improve metabolism and create on-demand energy.

The Three-Hour Rule: 24 Hours*				
7:00 A.M.	**10:00** A.M.	**12:30** P.M.	**3:30** P.M.	**7:00** P.M.
Breakfast	Snack	Lunch	Snack	Dinner

*Allow for a 10- to 12-hour nightly fast

Step 5: Calories

We have not talked about calories at all up until this point. It's now time to turn our attention to quantity or caloric intake. One key we want you to know is that all calories are not created equal. One hundred calories of chocolate cake does not equal 100 calories of broccoli. With that being said, the number of calories a person consumes is also extremely important. You can consume the right types of foods and beverages, but if you consume too much at any one time, then your health will suffer. Moderating a diet with high-quality nutrients is the sustainable way to maintain optimal health and performance.

How Many Calories Should You Consume Each Day?

The number of calories most people need each day depends on many factors such as your activity level, lean muscle mass, stress, and frequency of meals. Your daily calorie needs may vary, depending on how your day unfolds. Have you ever experienced days when you just can't get filled up, where you feel like you are starving all day long? Do you have other days when you are not that hungry? The following list gives a range of calories to work with; remember, this is a just a range. Your goal is not to count calories, but to have an awareness of the quantity of the foods and beverages you consume. Listen to your body and its nutritional needs!

Calories Ranges Per Day

Adult female: 1,500–2,500 calories
Adult male: 1,750–3,500 calories

Step 6: The 80/20 Rule

Now the hard part begins—making your *EAT* habits stick. Imagine developing a lifestyle that you truly enjoy—a lifestyle that gives more than it receives each and every day. The 80/20 rule is not about being perfect nor is it meant to be restrictive. The 80/20 rule is a range or guideline to follow: 80 percent of the time you are focused and dialed in, and 20 percent of the time you can take a few liberties whenever you feel the need. If you want a beer or glass of wine, dessert, or whatever you're craving, there's nothing wrong with enjoying it. Leave the guilt in the closet! Many people ask questions along the lines of "Do you have a cheat day?" This type of thinking indicates a very restrictive diet for six days of the week—no fun, little satisfaction, and just counting down the hours until you can indulge and engorge for an entire day. If we want to eat or drink something that is a little out of bounds, then so be it. The goal is to develop a nutritional plan that is yours—one that you enjoy, that is repeatable, and that accomplishes all of your health goals.

The below chart is an example of the 80/20 rule. When people look at it this way they realize they most likely have been on the

50/50 plan. This is not a bad thing, but it makes it very hard to progress. If you are looking for change, and sustainable change, the 80/20 rule is your key to success.

The basic idea is that four meals out of the week or six days out of the month you can splurge; this is your 20 percent. Remember to be intentional about your choices and mindful about how much and how often you indulge. Food is an experience and it's meant to be enjoyed in every way. In a given month you average around 84 meals and a given week you average 21 meals a week. Below is a look at a 21 meal week. You will notice that four meals are marked. These are the meals that are part of the 20 percent the rest are high quality meals making up the 80 percent.

Monday	Tuesday	Wednesday	Thursday	Friday	Saturday	Sunday
Breakfast	Breakfast	Breakfast	Breakfast	Breakfast	Breakfast	Breakfast
Lunch	Lunch	Lunch	Lunch	Lunch	Lunch	Lunch
Dinner	Dinner	Dinner	Dinner	Dinner	Dinner	Dinner

The Power of Food

What you eat and drink on a daily basis can change your life and the life of your organization. It is easy to understand that if a person is highly medicated, overweight, sleep deprived, and too sedentary, then capacity for growth and creativity will diminish. We have worked with thousands of people over the years who deal with myriad chronic conditions through medication. If we could start to empower each employee to take charge of their own health, the performance improvement would be exponential.

Today, thousands of people now have the knowledge, skills, and belief that their productivity is influenced on what and how they eat. *EAT* is a foundational pillar for you or your organization's success.

The bottom line is that diets, fads, and trends will never work. Short-term fixes will not give you long-term results. Building capacity starts with a healthy lifestyle full of high-quality foods and beverages. Figure 9.6 represents five sample days, based on quality.

BEST SAMPLE DAY

Drink 1/2 body weight in ounces of water/day (Ex: 150 lbs = 75 ounces of water)
6:00 am Wake up, stretch, water, eliminate
6:15 am Wheatgrass ice cubes (2-5 ice cubes)
6:30 am MOVE (Exercise)
8:00 am 1-2 tbsp. Cod liver oil with glass of lemon water
8:30 am Breakfast: Oatmeal on the go (add ½ cup raw oats, ½ cup almond milk, 1 tsp. cinnamon, 2 tbsp. raisins, 2 tbsp. almonds/walnuts to a plastic container and put in refrigerator overnight).
11:30 am Snack: Banana, raw macadamia nuts, and spirulina/chlorella (10 tablets)
1:00 pm Lunch-Large salad with veggies, hemp seeds and homemade vinaigrette, 10 minutes of sunlight
4:00 pm Snack: Smoothie (add frozen fruit, spinach, carrot juice, coconut water, cacao nibs, and chia seeds to a blender & mix), and spirulina/chlorella (10 tablets)
5:00 pm MOVE (Exercise if no morning workout)
6:00 pm 1 glass of mineral water with lime while preparing dinner
7:00 pm Dinner: Grilled chicken/salmon, baked broccoli, baked red-skin potato, or sweet potato
10:00 pm-6:00 am: 7-8 hours planned sleep

BETTER SAMPLE DAY

Drink 1/2 body weight in ounces of water/day (Ex: 150 lbs = 75 ounces of water)
6:00 am Wake up, stretch, water, eliminate
6:15 am Wheatgrass ice cubes (2-5 ice cubes)
6:30 am MOVE (Exercise)
8:00 am 1-2 tbsp. Cod liver oil with glass of lemon water
8:30 am Breakfast: Free-range scrambled eggs with baby kale, organic goat cheese, and mushrooms
11:30 am Snack: Orange/apple, and spirulina/chlorella (10 tablets)
1:00 pm Lunch: Almond butter and banana on sprouted grain bread, carrot sticks
4:00 pm Snack: 2 tbsp. ground flaxseeds with ¼ cup of 100% Pomegranate juice, let sit 10 minutes before eating with a spoon, and spirulina/chlorella (10 tablets)
5:00 pm MOVE (Exercise if no morning workout)
6:00 pm 1 glass of mineral water with lemon while preparing dinner
7:00 pm Dinner- Baked wild-caught salmon, quinoa, and steamed Brussels sprouts
10:00pm- 6:00am: 7-8 hours planned sleep

FIGURE 9.6 Sample Days.

GOOD SAMPLE DAY

Drink 1/2 body weight in ounces of water/day (Ex: 150 lbs = 75 ounces of water)

6:00 am Wake up

6:30 am MOVE (Exercise)

8:00 am 1-2 tbsp. cod liver oil with glass of water

8:30 am Breakfast: Organic Greek yogurt with granola and fresh berries

11:30 am Trail mix (nuts and dried fruit)

1:00 pm Lunch: Tuna salad/chicken salad/egg salad on whole grain bread, hummus and vegetables

4:00 pm Sliced apple lightly drizzled with raw honey and cinnamon, and spirulina/chlorella (10 tablets)

7:00 pm Dinner: Turkey burgers with organic cheese and avocado on whole grain bun, with side salad

11:00pm- 6:00am: 6-7 hours planned sleep

FAIR SAMPLE DAY

8:30 am Breakfast: Maple & brown sugar instant oatmeal

11:30 am Pretzels

1:00 pm Lunch: Grilled cheese and tomato soup

4:00 pm Corn chips and salsa

7:00 pm Lasagna and garlic bread

12:00am- 6:00am: 5-6 hours of sleep

POOR SAMPLE DAY

Drink 1/2 body weight in ounces of water/day (Ex: 150 lbs = 75 ounces of water)

6:00 am Wake up

7:00 am No breakfast

11:30 am Donut

1:00 pm Peanut butter and jelly sandwich on white bread, potato chips

4:00 pm Candy bar

7:00 pm Fast food meal, soda pop

8:00 pm Microwave popcorn

1:00am- 6:00am: 4-5 hours of sleep

FIGURE 9.6 Sample Days. (Continued)

Fun Diet Facts

- Over 100 million Americans adults diet every year.
- 1903: President William Howard Taft pleads to lose weight after getting stuck in the White House bathtub.
- The average American male weighed 165 pounds in 1960; today he weighs 200 pounds. Women have gone from 140 to 175 pounds.
- 10 is the age 80 percent of girls start dieting.
- 1975: A Florida doctor created the Cookie Diet.
- 1977: Slim-Fast created shakes for breakfast, lunch, and dinner.
- 1980s: The high-carb, low-fat diet reigned.
- 1991: Americans go high protein, low carb, and low fat.
- 2000s: The high-protein, low-carb, diet with a little fat became popular.
- 2010: The high-protein, low-carb, high-fat diet was all the rage.
- Four out of 10 people are considered obese in the US today.

We must take control of our health starting today. This dieting thing is not working.

Key Point

Does your current nutrition plan support the three On Target Living principles? For a full understanding of these principles, please visit: http://ontargetliving.com/3-principles.

Three Principles:
1. Cell health
2. pH balance
3. Source

10 *MOVE*

Why exercise? Have you ever wondered how did formal exercise or movement begin and why? Since the beginning of time it was necessary for humans to use their bodies for transportation, for physical work, to fight, to run from predators, to climb; we had to move to survive.

If we take a journey back in time to the days of the Roman gladiators, it becomes apparent why the gladiators started training specifically to get fitter, faster, and stronger—it was all about survival. For over 650 years the gladiators and their trainers were some of the first to understand training for optimal strength and elite performance. Today it is not necessary to train like the gladiators of our past, but as our demands continue to increase at a rapid pace, it becomes increasingly necessary to *move* daily for greater health, performance, and to build our capacity.

When I (Chris) entered Michigan State University as an exercise physiology graduate student in the early 1980s, my class schedule included the basic sciences such as anatomy, chemistry, and physiology. Then came my first exercise physiology class, and it was a game changer for me. Exercise physiology is the science of speeding up the processes that occur in the human body under stress and under demands, and of the acute responses and chronic adaptations that occur in the human body and mind under a variety of taxing conditions. I became fascinated at how the body adapts under the right training conditions. Given the right formula of movement, adequate rest, and proper nutrition, the mind and body will adapt and get stronger; bottom line, your ability to handle more under greater demands increases—your functional capacity expands!

On the opposite side of the spectrum, I was shocked by how quickly the human body can also break down with too much or too little movement. Did you know that too much movement could also break down the mind and body? As physical and emotional demands exceed capacity, stress hormones such as epinephrine and cortisol may quickly rise, leading to a decline in your building hormones—growth hormone and testosterone. These building hormones are essential for growth and repair. Did you also know that after only 14 days of complete bed rest, the human body loses over 50 percent of its functional capacity? The human body is magical in its ability to heal itself and get stronger with the right formula of *resting*, *eating*, and *moving*!

Exercise Is Good for *You*

By now almost everyone knows that regular movement or exercise is good for you. We will use movement or exercise in the same context throughout the rest of this chapter. The surgeon general reports that a sedentary lifestyle carries the same risk as smoking, high blood pressure, type 2 diabetes, or an imbalanced cholesterol profile. The research on the benefits of daily movement is overwhelming; in addition to making people happier, daily exercise improves mood, increases energy and engagement, improves sleep, decreases stress, improves heart health, decreases the risk of cancer and type 2 diabetes, improves bone health, keeps weight under control, improves strength and flexibility, improves sex life, increases brain power and memory, boosts the immune system, improves digestion—the list is long and will continue to increase.

The number-one reason we want you to move your body on a daily basis is how it can make you feel during and after exercise. Your mind becomes clear, your body feels loose and relaxed, and you feel energized and alive. Have you ever had a bad day, lots on your mind, too much stress, nothing seems to be working? Then you move your body and you feel refreshed and energized? Movement washes your brain; no longer do things bother you as much, your energy is up, and you feel great! Don't take us the wrong way; we want you to look fit and trim. But it is the experience and feeling you get when exercising that keeps you going back. Most people keep coming back to exercise because they enjoy the process—finding enjoyment in movement is critical for long-term success and sustainability!

What Is Holding *You* Back?

If daily movement or exercise came in pill form, it would be the most prescribed medication in the world! Yet, even with all this knowledge, research, and promotion, people around the world are moving less. Given everything we know, why are we not exercising or moving more? Based on our 30-plus years of health and fitness consulting, speaking around the world, and talking with seminar attendees, friends, family, physicians, and colleagues, we believe there are five major reasons why many people are not exercising on a regular basis: values and beliefs, lack of knowledge, insufficient time, not enjoying the process, and no developed rituals.

1. Values and Beliefs

We all have different values and beliefs in all aspects in our lives. Values differ from beliefs. You may value your health but believe you need to spend hours in the gym to become healthy or need lots of cardio to lose weight. For a good portion of our society, exercise is low on the priority list. For many it is not even on the radar screen. We believe most people recognize exercise or movement is a good thing, but something is holding them back. They may feel intimidated, uncomfortable with their body, or fearful they may fail.

Exercise can be magical and life changing. Exercise can improve your ability to move; prevent injuries; decrease aches and pains; decrease stress; improve your fitness, strength, and flexibility; improve your mood and mental clarity; increase your energy; help you sleep better; and improve your health. If you polled a group of people, most would say their health is of great importance to them. They value their health, and why not? When you don't have your health, you don't have much!

How valuable is your health to you? If you believe your health is important to you, what are you willing to do to maintain or improve your health? Make daily movement or exercise a priority in your life. Value your health and believe you are worth it!

2. Lack of Knowledge

Many people lack knowledge about what exercises or movements to do, how to start, how much exercise is enough, and most importantly how to get your exercise plan going. You might want to challenge me. You might be thinking, "Are you kidding me? Everywhere I look there are books, magazines, videos, websites, podcasts, webinars, and infomercials dedicated to exercise." Just like nutrition, there is so much information, good and bad, that people are overwhelmed. Many people are confused about whether to do high- or low-intensity cardio to lose weight and what specific strength training exercises will sculpt or shape a certain body part. What types of exercises can I do if I have bad knees, pain in my shoulder, chronic back pain, or type 2 diabetes? What exercises should I avoid? What exercises would be beneficial? Do I have the correct exercise technique?

Having the right knowledge will allow you to pivot on demand. This is one reason we recommend hiring a health and fitness coach to help educate and guide you on developing an exercise or movement plan that works for you. Whether you have a bad back or pain in your shoulder, or want to lose weight, learn how do a correct push-up, improve your numbers, or get into the best shape of your life, there are many terrific health and fitness coaches to help you reach your goals.

3. Insufficient Time

Time is a big issue for almost everyone. We want to make this point extremely clear: *you can never out-exercise a poor diet!* Most people do not have to spend large amounts of time to stay healthy and get into good shape. If you are training for a triathlon, marathon, or the Olympics, then, yes, you do have to invest large amounts of time to reach your goals. If your goal is to build your capacity, get healthier and in better shape, you will get the most out of your exercise program and achieve your goals if you adjust the frequency, quality, and amount of time you schedule for exercise.

At the beginning of each new year, we see so many people desperately trying to get in better shape. "This is my year!" One of the biggest mistakes most people make is believing that the more time they spend on exercise, the greater their results will be. Spending more time on the treadmill or in the gym does not necessarily add up to greater results. This is a huge mistake that we believe is a large reason why most people slowly abandon their exercise programs: it takes up too much time, making it almost impossible to sustain. We are not saying you can't have greater focus and intensity at certain times of the year with your *REST*, *EAT*, and *MOVE* plans, but is this something that you can sustain? Do you want to run a sprint or a marathon? We want you to think of movement or exercise as compound interest—your goal is to deposit into your health bank account on a daily basis. How can you incorporate daily movement into your already busy life? Can you carve out 10 minutes each day for the rest of your life to devote to daily movement? We want you to get into a mindset that you need to move your body every day. The human body is designed to move on a daily basis. Your time is precious and you don't need to spend lots of time exercising—the key is moving your body every day so you keep building up your health account!

4. Not Enjoying the Process

We have become a society that wants everything now. We seek instant gratification. Many of the wonderful benefits from daily movement come later, in the form of delayed gratification. Lowered blood pressure, balanced cholesterol, lower body fat, improved fitness, greater strength and flexibility, a better night's sleep, stronger bones—you don't reap all of these benefits overnight. There have been many times when we just don't feel like moving our bodies; we are busy or tired. We have all the excuses too. When we feel like this, we focus on how we will feel during the middle of the exercise activity and how we will feel when we are done exercising. For us these are two powerful motivators. In the middle of our exercise routine, our hearts are pumping, the body is sweating, energy has increased, and the body feels alive. After exercise, energy is high, the mind is clear, the body feels loose, and mood is great. The feelings from exercise are priceless.

The most difficult time for many is just getting started—we call this the three-minute rule. In most cases after three short minutes, energy begins to improve, your brain becomes clear, your heart rate begins to climb, and the benefits continue to pile up!

One of the key motivators for developing a sustainable exercise program is finding movement activities you enjoy—enjoying the process is the gold nugget most people overlook. Walking, running, biking, swimming, playing tennis, yoga, Pilates, skiing, strength training, pickleball, paddleball, playing basketball, playing soccer, dancing, surfing—finding a movement activity you enjoy is paramount to your success! We believe teaching people how to enjoy moving their body is essential for sustainable movement. If people don't enjoy their movement activities, they most likely will not continue. Many people have never experienced the joy of learning how to use their body!

We once trained a couple. The woman loved coming to the gym and working out, but her husband did not feel the same way. He did not like coming to the gym. We kept asking him is there an activity or sport he would like to try? He said yes, "I would like to learn how to play basketball." At age 73, this man had never played basketball before. The next day we went to the gym and rolled out the basketballs. We showed him how to dribble, pass, and shoot layups; he even took a few three-point shots and crazy as it sounds, he made his first shot from behind the arch! The laughter between him and his wife was heartfelt. We developed a plan that increased his capacity on the court; he worked on his balance, strength, flexibility, and agility. He now had a purpose for his workouts and most importantly enjoyed the process. Learning how to enjoy the process can be magical!

5. No Developed Rituals

What is a ritual? A ritual is something that becomes part of you, like your DNA. A behavior starts as a focused thought, and then moves into a habit, and over time may become a ritual. A ritual is something you do on a regular basis without much thought. This is one reason it is so difficult for people to quit smoking. It has become a powerful ritual. You have a cup of coffee—you have a cigarette. You read the newspaper—you have a cigarette.

Brushing your teeth, taking a shower, getting dressed, putting your shoes on the same way each and every day are powerful rituals. If you are not moving your body on a daily basis how then do you develop an exercise ritual? What do you want? Why do you want it? How are you going to do it? Start slowly and focus on two factors, time and enjoyment. This is one reason we have most of our clients walk for 10 minutes and do a series of yoga poses for five minutes every day. It does not take much time; incorporates balance, strength, flexibility, and fitness all rolled into one; can be done virtually anywhere; and makes clients feel great. We can always add more exercises or movement activities later, but first we want them to develop some movement rituals that will last. Imagine moving your body on a daily basis for the rest of your life. Developing healthy rituals is one of the keys to a healthy and happier you.

Movement and Weight Loss

Before we jump into the specific exercise portion of the chapter, we want to discuss weight loss and the mindset associated with successful weight loss. Many people we encounter at On Target Living have a specific goal of losing weight and believe that they will lose weight if they exercise or just move more. The truth is, it is not that simple. You will burn more calories and maybe lose a few pounds by moving more, but many people who exercise regularly are still overweight due to their poor nutritional habits. Many people still believe that long-duration, low-intensity cardiovascular exercise in the best method to lose weight, thinking the more calories they burn, the more weight they will lose. Unfortunately for many, spending more of their precious time in the pursuit of losing weight is not efficient or effective.

The latest research has shown that higher intensity bursts of cardiovascular exercise is much more efficient and effective in stimulating the lean hormones that aid in weight loss. However, although high intensity cardiovascular can be effective in getting the body in better shape, it can be very difficult, unpleasant, and extremely challenging to sustain. This type of high-intensity training is not much fun, and most people will not enjoy the process, which leads to greater stress. A more successful approach to movement or exercise takes into account enjoyment and learning how to pivot and perfect the activities you enjoy.

Chris's Story

For over 30 years I have competed in natural bodybuilding. My first contest was in 1985, and have competed in 10 since with the latest being in 2013. Every year I compete people ask, "What type of exercise program do you do to get into that type of shape on stage"? I would tell them that my workouts are relatively the same all year long. My intensity and focus is greater prior to competition, but my workout routine does not change a great deal prior to the contest. But nutritionally everything tightens up. I fast for over 12 hours or more each night (7:00 P.M. to 7:00 A.M.), drink plenty of water, take my superfoods, and eat more frequently throughout the day. My portion sizes are smaller, and I eat in the center of the Food Target for three months before a competition. This is not the 80/20 rule, but the 99/1 plan. I enjoy the challenge and the process, but it is difficult to sustain long term.

Proper nutrition accounts for 80–85 percent of successful weight loss. Clean up your diet, move your body daily, get enough rest; this is the magic formula for sustainable weight control.

This is an example of the before and after (Figures 10.1a and 10.1b). The exercise routine is almost identical; the nutritional program is what tightens up. You can't out train a bad diet.

10.1A Chris Before (January 2002, age 45)

10.1B Chris After (April 2002, age 45)

New Movement Mindset

A few years ago on a family vacation in northern Michigan, we took a trip over to the Pierce Stocking Scenic Drive, the Empire State Building of sand dunes. This sand dune rises 450 vertical feet, straight up out of Lake Michigan. The view of Lake Michigan from the top is incredible; you are so high you feel as if you are looking out of an airplane. The sign at the top cautions any climber who is thinking of climbing down to Lake Michigan to think seriously about turning back due to the steepness of this sand dune and the fact that it may take multiple hours to get back up. The sand dune was so enticing—it was almost begging you to take the challenge and climb down to the bottom.

We all decided to take the plunge and climb down into this steep beast. The climb down was nothing but exhilarating! The sand was deep, and the dune was so steep that with each step you felt as though you could fly. We were all laughing like a bunch of little kids frolicking to the bottom. When we arrived at the bottom and all of us looked up, we knew why there was a severe caution sign at the top. As we looked back up the steep sand dune, you could see people everywhere; the sand was littered with people trying to make their way back up and many were not moving—they were just lying in the sand, totally exhausted. On the way down we did not notice the people lying in the sand; we were too busy laughing and enjoying the ride down. One by one we headed back up. The sand was deep and for each step we took, it felt like we were barely moving upward. The climb up was exhausting but we all felt a sense of accomplishment that we did it. Matt said to me, "Imagine, dad, if most people could complete this climb. How would this impact our spending on health care, our health, our performance, our capacity? What would our world look like if everyone moved his or her body on a daily basis?"

Rolling Back the Hands of Time

We don't want to suggest that there is only one specific way to move your body, or that the exercises we discuss in this book are the only means to achieve the results you are seeking. Our recommendations are meant to be a jumping off point for someone new to exercise or a way to enhance those of you that are experienced exercisers.

Let's begin by asking a few questions: Are you currently exercising or moving your body on a daily basis? How would you rate your current fitness level on a 1–10 scale? What would you like your current fitness to be? What type of investment would it take to accomplish your health and fitness goals? What type of exercises or movements do you enjoy? Do you have any injuries that are holding you back from activities you used to enjoy? Would you like to participate in these activities once again?

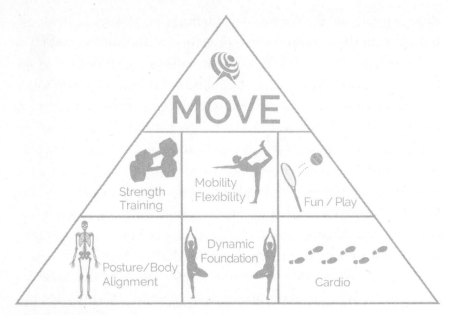

FIGURE 10.2 MOVE Methodology

Start slowly, train smart, and choose ways to move your body on a daily basis that are fun, enjoyable, and repeatable. We have outlined a sequence of movement steps (Figure 10.2) that can create outstanding results and help us all turn back the hands of time.

MOVE Methodology

Step 1: Posture/Body Alignment

Step 1 begins with learning how to improve your posture and body alignment. Almost all muscular/skeletal problems begin with poor posture and an imbalance of our body alignment. When the body slowly gets out of alignment, many injuries start to show up. Back pain; foot, ankle, knee, and hip pain; neck and shoulder problems; and many more issues stem from poor posture and poor body alignment. For example, if you round your shoulders and drop your head forward while working on your computer, sitting at your desk, driving your car, walking, or using a cardiovascular machine or during strength training, the rotator cuff—the muscles that work in harmony moving the shoulder—can easily become impinged and damaged. When you sit up straight, elevate the chest, and drop the shoulder blades down and in, the space in the shoulder joint increases, allowing the rotator cuff tendons to easily glide back and forth, moving the shoulder in harmony with increased range of motion and no pain. The five key points for ideal posture alignment are the ear, shoulder, hip, knee, and ankle. (See Figure 10.3.)

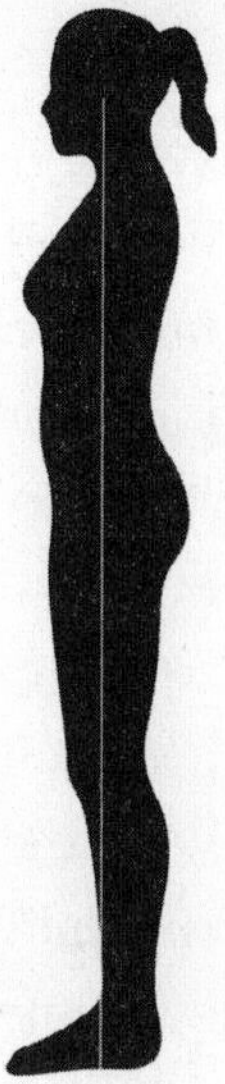

We all get into movement patterns, and over time, certain muscles become shorter and many times stronger, while opposing muscles may become weaker. This can create muscle imbalances

FIGURE 10.3 Ideal Posture

that lead to poor posture, an increase of injuries, pain, and a loss in mobility and flexibility. Training the nervous system with specific exercises can improve posture and body alignment. Here are two easy posture exercises that take seconds to perform and that you can do each and every day:

- Standing wall extension—Stand tall with your heels, butt, shoulders, and head against the wall and slowly raise your arms overhead. Do this three to five times.
- Standing upward dog and downward dog—Place your hands on your desk or wall. Keep your arms straight, stick your rear end up and out, and slowly stand up arching your back. Do this three to five times.

Let's all begin to fight back in our battle against gravity by improving our posture. Paying attention to your posture and body alignment can go a long way in keeping the body healthy and performing at its best.

Step 2: Move Your Body Daily

We believe many people don't move or exercise because they feel like they don't have enough time. You don't need a lot of time to improve your health, fitness, and performance. Think of movement or exercise as compound interest—you need to deposit every day into your health bank account. Take the stairs, stretch at your desk or at the airport, go for a walk, or do a set of body-weight squats or push-ups; even if you have just five minutes to move, do it! If your goal is to have more energy, increase your focus, improve your mood, then start moving. Remember, *motion creates positive emotion*! Changing your mindset to include moving your body evry day can reap great benefits over time.

Step 3: Flexibility and Balance

As we age our flexibility and balance can quickly disappear if we do not work at it. Can you easily touch your toes? Stand on one foot and hold for 10 seconds? What many people are missing in their daily movement or exercise plan is flexibility and balance. As your flexibility and balance improve, so does your ability to move with ease and grace. Aches and pains slowly start to disappear, and your body begins to feel more supple and young again. There are many wonderful exercises to improve flexibility and balance—the key is devoting just a few minutes each day working to improving your flexibility and balance. We have outlined a series of exercises that will improve your posture, flexibility, balance, and overall health and fitness in less than 8–10 minutes per day.

Dynamic Warm-Up (2 to 3 minutes)

We use the dynamic warm-up exercises at the beginning of all our exercise sessions (see Figure 10.4). The dynamic warm-up exercises cover the entire body, lubricate the joints, improve flexibility and balance, and are quick, taking less than two to three minutes

FIGURE 10.4 Dynamic Warm-Up Exercises

to perform. Use slow and controlled movements and gradually increase the range of motion as you warm up.

- Arm swing
- Neck stretch (side to side, rotation)
- Side bend
- Trunk twist
- Front leg swing
- Side leg swing

Foundation Exercises (5 to 6 minutes)

We call the foundation exercises the *superfoods of movement*. The foundation exercises are a series of yoga movements that can improve your posture, balance, flexibility, strength, and fitness, all rolled into a five- to six-minute movement routine (see Figure 10.5). Hold each movement for two to five seconds and focus on the proper form along with your breathing. Experiment, challenge yourself, make mistakes, and enjoy the wonderful benefits they can bring.

FOUNDATION EXERCISES

squat — straight-leg lunge — warrior 3 — half moon

warrior 1 — warrior 2 — reverse warrior — extended angle

spread eagle — dancer — standing downward dog — standing upward dog

FIGURE 10.5 Foundation Exercises

- Centering squat
- Straight-leg lunge—warrior III—half moon
- Warrior 1—warrior 2—reverse warrior—extended angle—spread eagle
- Dancer
- Standing upward dog and downward dog
- Half-moon (against the wall)

Step 4: Strength Training

If there is one form of movement that can turn back the hands of time, it is strength training. The benefits of strength training include increased strength, increased bone density, improved mobility and functionality, improved posture, better balance, increased athletic performance, injury prevention, reduced stress, increased self-esteem, increased metabolism, weight control, improved overall health, and increased capacity. Strength training truly is the Fountain of Youth.

Strength training can be done using a variety of equipment such as free weights, kettlebells, resistance bands, machines, or your own body weight. Here are few guidelines to follow:

1. Posture/body alignment—Begin each movement with a good foundation, and try to maintain good posture throughout each exercise. If your form begins to break down, stop the exercise or movement.
2. Technique—Are you performing the movement correctly? If you are performing the exercise with poor mechanics, you may be reinforcing an unhealthy movement pattern. We highly recommend hiring a health professional to help you perfect your strength training movements.
3. Progressions—There is more to strength training than repetitions, sets, and resistance. Allow your body time to adapt to your strength training exercises. As your body begins to adapt to your strength-training program, start making a few small changes in your program so your body stays challenged and continues to make adaptations. There are seven areas of progressions that you can change on demand. They include the:
   - Number of exercises
   - Number of sets
   - Number of repetitions
   - Amount of resistance
   - Length of rest and recovery
   - Speed of movement
   - Stability and balance (e.g., lifting your feet in the air while doing a dumbbell bench press)

4. Breathing—Your breath helps you monitor the intensity level of each exercise. As the intensity of the exercise rises, you may find you are starting to hold your breath. Try to maintain a consistent breathing pattern throughout all of your strength exercises.

5. Perfect the ordinary—Imagine if you and everyone in your organization could do one perfect bodyweight squat and one perfect push-up; how fit would you be? How fit would your organization be? The key for staying healthy and fit is to focus on a few basic movements and perfect the ordinary.

Here are a few of our favorite strength-training exercises:

- Squat (bodyweight or dumbbells)
- Step back or step up
- Ankle-tubing side step
- Psoas hip raise (Tip: Helps with sciatic nerve pain)
- Push-up (modified or regular)
- Pull-up or lat pull-down
- Standing bodyweight row
- Standing shoulder press
- Standing flexion/extension

Step 5: Cardio

Cardiovascular exercise includes walking, hiking, jogging, biking, swimming, cross-country skiing—virtually any movement that is rhythmic in nature and gets the heart pumping. There are many benefits of cardiovascular exercise, including stress reduction, improved pH balance, improved cellular sensitivity, mood elevation, increased cardiovascular efficiency, improved blood pressure, improved blood glucose, cholesterol balance, and weight control. Bottom line: It helps you feel good and expands your capacity.

Here are a few guidelines to follow:

1. Modality—Find a cardio movement you enjoy and add variety to your exercise plan. Do you enjoy swimming; walking; running; biking; playing tennis, paddleball, or basketball; skiing; taking a group fitness class; or using a cardiovascular machine or mini-trampoline? The key for sustainable fitness is finding an activity you enjoy.
2. Frequency—Try to raise your heart rate two to six times per week.
3. Duration—This is the big one: you can never out-exercise a poor diet. We find many people spend way too much time doing cardiovascular exercise in the hope of losing weight. Cardiovascular exercise is a very inefficient method to losing weight. All you need for improved health and greater capacity is 10–25 minutes of high-quality cardiovascular exercise. If you want to go on a long walk or bike ride, no problem, but get out of the mindset that you need to spend your precious time doing lots of cardio.
4. Intensity—Cardio does not have to be painful to be beneficial. Get your heart rate up, and try to get a little uncomfortable; it's okay to get out of breath, but cardio does not have to be extremely intense to be beneficial. Remember, the key for sustainable movement is enjoying the process.

Step 6: Play/Fun

We all need to play more and enjoy moving more. Play contributes to the cognitive, physical, social, and emotional well-being of kids and adults. Today more than ever before our society has become over structured, especially when it comes to play. Sit back and listen when people are free playing; you hear laughter. You can feel the joy flowing through the body; energy is high, people's moods are elevated, and stress of our fast-paced world seems to disappear. Take time to play and experience the tremendous benefits you, your friends and family, and your organization can enjoy by playing more.

Developing a movement plan begins by recognizing the tremendous benefits daily movement can bring to you and your organization. Moving your body on a daily basis can have magical benefits to your body and mind. Make your movement plan enjoyable fun, play more, perfect the ordinary, and remember that motion creates positive emotion. Let's get moving!

Figure 10.6 shows the exercise routines we help design for people.

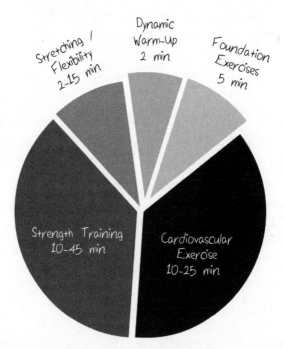

FIGURE 10.6   Sample exercise routine

Go Time

Now it's time to take action, to start moving on a daily basis. As mentioned, there are endless ways to move the human body—the key is to find a movement activity you enjoy and get your body in motion. Remember, motion creates positive emotion! Also, there is no one right way to move your body; the key is daily movement and then try to perfect the ordinary! Following the MOVE methodology can guide you and build a sustainable foundation that can easily be implemented throughout your entire organization. Start slowly and continue to upgrade your exercise habits.

Key Point

Exercise is great, but *movement* is essential. Think about moving your body daily.

11 *You* Have the Power

Most people don't take action.

You have, and always have had, the power. What are you going to do with it? Are *you* going to take action?

When we were developing this book, we wanted to include a chapter to show people how much power and influence they have on their organization, their life, and the things that matter most to them.

No matter whether you are a new associate, an intern, the CEO, an entrepreneur, a consultant, a contractor, or even someone who is ready to retire, you always have the power to influence others and make a positive impact. You have the power.

One of the limiting beliefs and attitudes we see in organizations and with their people is the attitude of "I/we have tried this before, and it didn't work." This type of thinking and attitude is why we wanted to write this chapter. Over the last several chapters, we gave you a glimpse into *why* and *how* you can get the desired outcomes you want—the methodology, the process, and the secret sauce. Processes always take time, and the one thing we can't control is the time it takes to reach an outcome. Changing the belief so you understand that *you* have the power allows you to see change that can take shape effortlessly across the most important elements of your organization and even your life.

Matt's *Power* Shift

This thinking changed for me when I was 18 years old. I had always been labeled a bad student, not very smart, not focused, afflicted with ADHD, and so on. These external labels shaped my beliefs of what the future might hold. Fortunately for me, I didn't completely lose hope; I always had an inner drive to get what I desired. One of my strongest desires was to play college golf. This was a burning desire that allowed me to overcome the limited skills or abilities that would prevent most people from going to college. As a student with a 2.6 GPA and a subpar 18 ACT score, I had to use my golf ability to get into college. You might be wondering, "How does this work? How do you get into college with these poor grades?" When you don't have the standard accepted grades and scores, you go through what is called a *special exemption.* This exemption is something that schools offer for students who possess other traits that could represent the school well, but don't have the accepted grades for general enrollment. Once accepted by the board, the school establishes requirements. You have to meet with an adviser once a week during your first year. Luckily my adviser was Dr. Damon Arnold. Dr. Arnold was a student-athlete academic adviser who was responsible for making sure student-athletes had all the resources to succeed in school.

This relationship allowed me to realize I had the power. Up until this point, I was convinced I was just bad at reading and writing, couldn't pay attention in class, and wasn't very smart. I had a very fixed mindset—why try if I wasn't going to be able to do it anyway? My attitude was less than positive. After two to three months of looking over my grades, checking on my attendance, and providing resources for me, Dr. Arnold called me into his office one Tuesday morning. I figured this was going to be our typical meeting. To give you a visual of Dr. Arnold—he is a six-plus-foot, 200-pound chiseled steel ex–football player with a ponytail dreadlock hairstyle. Everyone loved him; he was extremely admired and respected and treated student-athletes with the upmost respect and courtesy. He was the smoothest, most collected guy I have ever met—soft-spoken and eloquent, but witty and cool.

This meeting was a little different. I could tell he was getting frustrated with me, not because I wasn't doing what he asked or missing meetings, but because I wasn't trying to reach my true potential.

He started with: "Matt, what are you doing here?"

I looked at him and like a typical 18-year-old, I said, "I have to be here."

He smiled and chuckled.

"You don't have to do anything. Playing college golf is a choice, going to college is a choice, how you improve yourself is a choice. You have all these choices. You don't have to be here."

He went on: "Why are you wasting your time and my time? You have a ton of ability, the power to do anything you want. Why aren't you using this power? Why aren't you applying your abilities?"

I had nothing to say. For the first time it finally clicked.

It was that *aha* moment. I realized I do have control, I do have the power. Why couldn't I get good grades? Why not have success academically and athletically? I realized maybe I should continue to be curious and strive to be the best person I can be.

This moment shifted my thinking and ultimately changed the way I went about life. I changed from *can't happen* to *anything can happen*. I went on to be an academic all-conference and athletic all-conference athlete. I learned how to be a good student and to change my mindset to I *have the power*.

After not seeing Dr. Arnold since graduation, I decided to call him in January 2016 to thank him and explain how much he meant to me and the impact he made in my life. After our conversation, I decided it would be neat to interview him for my podcast, *The Matt Johnson Performance Podcast*. One part of this interview that stuck with me was about *imagination*. I asked him what he thought about information and knowledge. I wanted his thoughts on the information overload we have in our society and the importance of learning and knowledge. He said "Matt," everybody talks about knowledge being king, and as a person with two master's degrees and a PhD, trust me I believe knowledge is vital, and I believe we must do more teaching and learning, but to me the game changer is imagination." He went on to share this story:

> When I was a kid in inner-city Cleveland, I remember spending a bunch of time going to Sears. I loved to go to Sears to sit on the riding lawn mowers dreaming and imaging how big yards and houses must be if you need this riding lawn mower to mow the grass. See, Matt, at this point in my life I was only familiar with yards that were 10-by-10 feet and people could cut using a push mower with no motor. This imagination was the first time I remember realizing the world was bigger than I thought and people have things I knew nothing about. This imagination drove me to want to see what else life had to offer, the true potential. This imagination allowed me to believe anything is possible. I now have a yard that requires a riding lawn mower.

I had never heard him tell this story and, looking back, I realized what he was truly asking me when I came into his office as an 18-year-old college kid was this, "What do you want your life to look like?"

If you can imagine it, it can happen. The critical piece was, I had to believe I had the power.

Just Because It Hasn't Happened Doesn't Mean It Won't Happen

We are here to not only tell you but ultimately show you how to use the power to improve the capacity of everything and everyone in your life.

It's almost too easy to dismiss any attempt to create positive change in the workplace. All organizations have cultures built around foundational attitudes and beliefs that are rarely challenged or questioned. We know everyone wants to do and be their best, but knowing and doing are completely different things. The perceived risks of rocking the boat likely outweigh any potential long-term benefits of changing the status quo. It's a safer move to toe the line and preserve your position within the organization, right? Why should you stick your neck out on the line, when no one listens to your ideas in the first place?

Most of us barely have time to slow down and assess a better way forward. Like all collective bodies, an organization or large group adopts a herd mentality to react to imminent and immediate threats to the bottom line. This vicious cycle leads to a culture that isn't armed for the future. We have illustrated the big five problems, the vision for the future, and the action you can take to get ahead of the competition, but are you going to act?

Before we start unpacking the different mindsets you need to execute this positive change in the workplace, we want to take a moment to think about all the monumental innovations that drove the last century of enormous economic, political, and social change in civil society—positive change on a colossal scale. The great titans of industry—Thomas Edison, Roy Firestone, and Henry Ford—come to mind, as do the tech scions of Silicon Valley: Steve Jobs, Mark Zuckerberg, and Elon Musk. They all have legacies built on creating millions of jobs, connecting billions of people, and launching infinite dreams. We imagine their ideas falling from a magical tree in a *eureka*—a single moment that suddenly launches them into a manic fury of experimenting and tinkering until they emerge from their labs rejoicing in the rapture of finally creating from scratch something brilliant and earth-shattering.

As much as we want to glorify the myth of the lone mad scientist, the idea of toiling away in a secret lab without any help or input from the outside world is fundamentally flawed. After trying hundreds of other filaments, Edison discovered that a special species of bamboo had a much higher resistance to electricity than other carbon paper–based materials deployed by dozens of early iterations of the light bulb. Xerox and its famed PARC research program had developed an early prototype of the computer mouse, but never could quite figure out how to apply the technology for consumers. Steve Jobs immediately recognized its potential to humanize the Macintosh—a distinction between invention and commercialization.

These prolific change agents did not spark paradigm shifts in a vacuum. Their success depended heavily on recognizing the right moments to stand on the shoulders of giants before them and bravely launch forward into a future only they could envision. They had to fight tirelessly to win hearts and minds. They had to articulate their brave new world in different ways for different audiences. They had to evangelize their arguments for a better way forward and influence countless cynics and skeptics to suspend their disbelief and invest in a more prosperous future for all. Most importantly, they never doubted their ability to be a catalyst for change. Be the matchstick for disruption.

Google rarely misses when it launches a new product line. Its legendary moonshots, fueled by the brightest minds at its X division, have fundamentally shaped the Information Age. The Silicon Valley mindset of "move fast and break things" ensures that every aspect of the final product has been refined by an ever-evolving feedback loop of iterative improvements. Google Glass was battle-tested in the lab and then put through its initial beta trial by thousands of new "Glass Explorers," who started sporting these head-mounted smartphone displays and ushered in a new age of ubiquitous computing.

It only took a few weeks of awkward face-to-face conversations and legitimate fears of strangers recording unsuspecting bystanders for these early adopters to be universally derided as "Glassholes." It only took a couple of months before developers created Google Glass apps that could steal smartphone passwords, take pictures with just the wink of an eye, or even record conversations without anyone noticing. In less than two years after the botched beta trials, Glass was pulled from the shelves and universally ridiculed as one of the worst product rollouts of the past 20 years.

Even the most successful companies are susceptible to ignoring the most important aspect of inspiring change: you have to alter attitudes first. On many different levels, from the interpersonal creepiness to highway safety, people's attitudes and beliefs about the dangers of in-your-face computing were already made up. Google believed that the functionality and novelty of the new device would overpower the public's preconceived notions about how it made them feel.

Change Is Hard

You have influence right now.

You have the power right now.

How are you using it?

In today's fast-paced economy, the desire to scale is at an all-time high. How can organizations or entrepreneurs be successful without scalable solutions? There are seven billion people in the world all with the opportunity to serve. Leadership inside these organizations looks to automate tasks in effort to reduce inefficiencies and scale growth further. One automation process that more and more organizations rely on is a CRM (customer relationship management) software. This tool is a marketing automation software that allows you to store data and communicate with prospective and current clients on a large scale. It also can automate commissions and track productivity.

Here's how integration often goes: With the new CRM software purchased and licensed, it's time to integrate it into the workforce. You assign your national sales manager to reveal the new process and system at the annual meeting in front of the top 500 sales leaders. The sales manager explains that all the manual tasks that have consumed so much of time up until this point are a thing of the past: "Today we start forging a better way forward to amplify our expansion into new markets and generate even more revenue from existing customers!"

The applause and confetti that leadership expected for this new direction is roundly doused with a sobering shower of confusion and doubt by every sales leader in the room. "Who's going to import all of my contacts into this new-fangled tool?" "How will commissions be split between two of my reps bidding on the same contract?" "How long will it take to transition to this new system?" "Why is this being jammed down our throats in the middle of our busiest quarter?!"

Resistance to new ideas is an innate human reaction to any perceived change in the ecosystem around them. Foreign concepts trigger an emotional response before any rational thought is rendered toward the idea itself. Sure, this new process or concept may very well increase productivity by eliminating redundancies, but logic has no bearing on attitudes and beliefs. People subconsciously make up their minds about new ideas before they're even presented.

Psychologists Muzafer Sherif and Carl Hovland proved this potent dynamic when they introduced social judgment theory in the late 1960s. According to this theory, our attitudes are graded on a continuum of pro to con based on our existing beliefs—which ultimately define our attitudes.

So how do you persuade your team to make the small changes necessary to realize the goals and outcomes envisioned? Is it even worth trying to convince those around you to move toward the same outcome if they all have vastly different attitudes and agendas? How do you build a coalition for change to begin with? It's easy to become overwhelmed by self-defeating thoughts when you step out from the crowd and try to pave an entirely new and different way forward. The following are a few questions you should ask yourself before planting the seeds of change.

1. Am I the Best Person to Deliver the Message?

Media approval ratings are at an all-time low, barely above big banks and Congress, according to the most recent public confidence poll from the Associated Press. The echo chambers created by a highly partisan 24-hour news cycle have conditioned the public to believe news organizations almost always have a political bias baked into every story they cover or publish. If you're a reporter working for a liberal newspaper and file a story on Planned Parenthood funding for a local health clinic, it will likely be perceived to have a favorable opinion of women's reproductive rights. A gun owner is almost always assumed to be in opposition of any gun control legislation. But what if a climatologist came forward and proposed that global warming is a fallacy perpetuated by corporations to drive sales of greener technology? You might listen more just to understand why their opinion is so drastically divergent from the rest of the scientific community.

The element of surprise, combined with a more appealing messenger, is a tried and true tactic for winning hearts and minds. What if the national sales manager from our earlier example called up the five best sales reps from the company and asked them to beta test the new CRM? Ultimately these marketing automation processes will benefit the reps on the ground the most. If a rep could automatically receive all new leads who attended a recent webinar, and know what type of content those leads viewed on the corporate site after listening, wouldn't they know exactly what types of solutions those leads were seeking? Instead of the new manager starting to sell the idea from the top down, let those who benefit the most show its results from the bottom up. Ultimately, a peer is going to listen and respond more positively to a 25 percent increase in revenue from his peer rep, than from the national sales manager who won't use this software nearly as much.

2. How Do I Convince Someone to Change Their Behavior?

We tend to gravitate toward people we already relate with. Opposites attract, but most healthy friendships and marriages persist and grow stronger because of parallel attitudes and beliefs. Social judgment theory calls this area the *latitude of acceptance*, but it is now commonly referred to as the *okay* zone. It's very important to respect your audience's zones of tolerance since any idea that falls outside these zones is highly likely to be rejected. If you walked up to someone in the store who was buying a bag of prepackaged cupcakes for their kids and shouted at them, "What are you doing? Are you stupid? How could you feed your children that processed garbage?" what would you expect them to do? Would they smile and say, "You know what, you're right. I can't believe I buy this stuff every week. Thanks for your concern!"? Or would they scowl and scream back, "How dare you tell me how to feed my children! Get away from me or I'm calling the cops!"? This is a bit of an extreme example, but it perfectly illustrates the wrong way to try and change an attitude that dictates daily habits and behaviors. The concern and passion for eating healthier food is on full display, but the vehement tone of judgment and condescension is immediately perceived as a threat to their children and a potential assault.

A better approach is to take the time to identify where someone's OK zone is before trying to persuade them in any given direction. According to Sherif and Hovland's research, people only change their minds within three degrees of where they sit on the latitude of acceptance. In other words, if you ask someone who has a neutral opinion on a topic, it's almost impossible for them to strongly agree with you right off the bat. They must slightly agree with your idea before they can even start to agree with it.

My dad has always been an avid golfer (he actually taught me how to play), but his swing mechanics still can use some fine-tuning from time to time. Heck, all our swings can use fine-tuning from time to time. He usually plays one to two times a week and hits on the range when he can. He has worked with a golf instructor regularly for the past three years, but still struggles to get off the tee with any consistency. Every year we play as partners in our club's invitational. It is a tradition for us, and we have played together for the last 10 years in a row. In the early years after he hit a bad shot, I would say things like "When did you start taking the club so inside on the backswing? That is why you hit it bad." This type of coaching does not work for him and tends to make him angry and question why would I say something like that—I'm not in the okay zone. I don't know what he has been working on, and I am sure he didn't intentionally try to swing incorrectly. This was not the way to help him make a change.

My new approach is using the okay zone. If I see some mechanics that need to change or something I believe could help him, I start of by asking, "What are you working on with your instructor?" This allows me to learn what he is working on and how he is thinking. Usually this conversation uncovers the challenges he is having and the feels he still doesn't have down. Once I uncover what he is working on and what he still is trying to figure out, I try to address these thoughts first. If he is struggling with his backswing, I don't tell him that his downswing is broken. I give him some specific cues that can allow him to make a better backswing. We all want to help, but helping someone change their behavior starts with them being in the okay zone.

3. How Do I Convince Large Groups of People to Change?

It's much easier to convince Chris to make small changes in his golf swing than to mobilize the momentum necessary for completely overhauling a company's processes and workflows. In order to create and sustain changes at a larger scale, we need to focus on the factors behind social influence and the key factors that determine the dynamics of how large groups interact. Social impact theory, developed by psychologist Bibb Latane in 1981, uses a relatively simple equation to predict the level of social impact for any given situation:

impact = strength × immediacy × number of people

Any good leader knows they can't advocate for change alone, but better leaders know they need to recruit the strongest supporters and create a sense of urgency to fuel the change they seek. Rarely does the entire company gather in a room to confront future challenges and create initiatives needed to deal with them. First, you must recruit a strong coalition of people who genuinely care and are willing to fight for change. When you do so, the chances of success increase exponentially.

So, let's go back to the national sales manager and his continued campaign to convince the sales team to adopt the new marketing automation processes. He's already won over the five best sales reps to start using lead generation to close more deals than they were before. Strength in numbers is already being attained, but the main ingredient missing is immediacy. As the national sales manager, Dave is always asked by the executives, "How are our competitors selling online and using automation?" So, this manager decides to block out a couple hours at the end of the week to visit some direct competitor sites and see if they're using any advanced marketing automation tactics to close more leads. It doesn't take long before he starts seeing the hallmarks of advanced marketing automation on full display: personalized content tailored to his clients; automated follow-up e-mails thanking him for signing up for their newsletter and a subsequent e-mail a couple of days later sharing blog articles that relate to his job title. He's heard rumors of how much one particular competitor had been eating into their market share, particularly for health-care clients. Dave visits the health-care segment page a few times during the day to see if he starts receiving e-mails related to those specific products. Sure enough, a couple of days later, he receives a personalized e-mail directly from the health-care rep in his region asking him if he had any questions about a recent whitepaper he downloaded about ADA (Americans with Disability Act) standards. Seeing firsthand how effective these tactics are, Dave forwards the e-mail chain to the five reps and asks them how long it normally takes to get someone this close to a sale. Within a few minutes, they reply back with varying degrees of concern and urgency, and they start to connect their diminishing market share in this space to how their rival is deploying these tactics.

The next morning, Dave receives an emergency meeting invite from all of the sales executives. He can't help but smile since he can sense the winds of change blowing in his favor, but he certainly doesn't want to count chickens before they hatch and takes a little time to prep himself on any possible objections they might have. Dave walks into the same conference room where before he was met with nothing but ridicule and suspicion and is greeted not only by the same executives but all five sales reps on the conference line. He sits down in disbelief. Not even he expected this type of coalition to materialize in a relatively short amount of time. He knows how hypercompetitive the reps are with each other, let alone the sales managers. He then hears a somewhat familiar voice dial in to the conference line and ask him a pointed question: "Dave, we haven't had the pleasure of meeting quite yet, but this is John Howard. Would you mind telling me a little more about this marketing automation tool and how you plan to help us implement it going forward?" Never in a million years did he imagine the president of his company would take the time to ask his opinion about anything. He tries to contain his excitement in his response, "Well, Mr. Howard, I never thought you'd ask."

You have the power to spark immense change within any organization. Like anything else in life, it's all about strategy and execution. The best part about being a change agent is actually experiencing just how green the grass is on the other side. Everyone around you is a little more optimistic about the future. They know that together, they can move mountains and accomplish big goals that improve not only their lives but also those around them.

The capacity for change is arguably the most defining and rewarding part of being alive. Humans have evolved over hundreds of thousands of years through a natural selection of better ideas over all else. It may sound cliché, but if you take change to heart and take the time to cultivate change to better those around you, the possibilities are truly limitless.

Take Action

Key Point

If you see a problem and you know the solution, you have the *power* to change anything!

12 Why *Not?*

Almost everything you read about being your best or creating the most amazing organizational culture begins and ends with finding your purpose, or what we call your *why*. Finding your why can be very powerful. However, there may be a consideration besides finding your *why* that triggers more action, that may guide you faster to where you should go. Have you ever asked yourself, *why not*?

Jim Collins, in his game-changing book *Good to Great*, ignited a tremendous paradigm shift when he redefined every organization's most valuable asset (its people). The analogy he used to personify this movement was filling up the bus (company/organization) with the right people and placing them in the right seats. His point was that your people are the most important part of your organization, and you need to build a process that finds and places the best people in the correct spot inside your organization.

Over the past 20 years since *Good to Great* came out, organizations and leaders have spent billions and billions of dollars recruiting, retaining, and evaluating their talent. Departments, committees, head hunters, managers, and corporate culture wizards have mastered this art. But is it enough for the future to just find and place the right people in the right seats? Does this talent need anything else? According to a 2017 Deloitte Human Capital Study "Rewriting the rules for the digital age,"[1] the past 20 years has yielded the worst increase in productivity in a very long time, yet technology is advancing at a vertical rate.

Jim Collins's principles will hold true to the test of time: Your people are the most valuable asset in your organization; continue to invest and refine your process to attract and retain talent. Where you have the biggest opportunity to differentiate yourself is by asking, "What is the most valuable asset to my people?" As you read in Chapter 2, your people's most valuable asset is their health. After you attract the right talent and place them in the right seats, your next thought should be, "How do I invest in this asset? What type of investment will give us and them the biggest return?" What we have unlocked over the last 10 years is that not only will the investment work for your current people, but when you invest in people where they need and want to be invested, you begin to attract and retain desirable recruits, and build the most unstoppable culture to fulfill the organizational purpose.

So, instead of asking, "Why should we build our people's capacity?" ask, "*Why not* build our people's capacity?" We all know our demands are increasing, so don't just rely on talent to handle drinking from the firehouse.

Oxygen Mask

It's hard not to roll your eyes and completely tune out during every airline safety demonstration. It's all common sense for the most part, right? Don't smoke in the lavatory. Make sure your tray tables are locked and your carry-on is stowed away during takeoff. If the oxygen masks are deployed due to loss of cabin air pressure, make sure to secure yours before helping others. That one always seemed second nature to us. Shouldn't people instinctively ensure their own safety and well-being before helping one another? That is a good

[1] https://www2.deloitte.com/content/dam/Deloitte/us/Documents/human-capital/hc-2017-global-human-capital-trends-us.pdf

analogy to explain the process of expanding your personal capacity and that of your organization. Put putting your own oxygen mask on first. The only difference is that, when it comes to capacity, there are a lot of other options.

When we travel and hear the message about putting the oxygen mask on before helping others, it makes us think, "Why don't people invest in themselves first? Why don't organizations see this urgency?" We all want to make an impact, help others, and be successful, but if we don't build our own capacity first, we are sacrificing the true potential to make a difference and to help others.

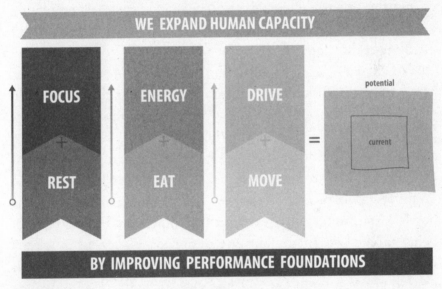

FIGURE 12.1 The Capacity Process.

Focus, energy, and *drive* are the oxygen of your organization (Figure 12.1). If you laid out all your goals, projects, and initiatives and asked, "What will we need from our people to crush these goals?" you will most likely come back to these three performance outcomes. Is it possible to be creative without focus? Can you make the sales and close the deals without energy? If you are trying to innovate, create, or adapt, will you have more drive than your competition?

In our fast-paced, cutthroat world it is easy to get caught up in the external noise, but if you truly want to help others and build the most amazing business, start by putting on the oxygen mask.

We Should All Be More Productive

In the age of instant access to everything all the time, shouldn't we be seeing record productivity? Smartphones, machine learning, and the advent of self-driving cars are just a few of the mind-blowing innovations that are marketed as productivity enhancers. These technological advances certainly create exciting opportunities for us, but they also enable us to create a vicious cycle of completion instead of capacity expansion. The Deloitte study highlights an alarming realization: We are not evolving like we could or should.

We talked about success in Chapter 1—everyone wants success. The area or specifics of success vary, but the drive to succeed is in all of us. It could be business, art, athletics, parenthood, friendship, philanthropy, economics, or anything you want. The true key to this success is productivity. Most believe productivity is to complete or to finish. We tell ourselves, "I was productive today. I got 10 things done, picked up the kids, made dinner, and washed the dog." What productivity really means is the state of or quality of being productive. In the burning desire to be successful, we are prioritizing finishing or completing; let's reprioritize quality. It is easy to create a to-do list and just check it off and think we are productive. In this hyperconnected superficial world, we should strive to be the best. When you think of success and productivity from now on, think about doing what you were meant to do with extreme quality. Over the course of this book we have given you the blueprint to expanding your capacity; this blueprint will take everything or anything you are doing and make it better so you can produce the quality that you are meant to.

Slack, smartphones, A/I, drivable cars, and so on are thought to be productivity enhancers. None of these affect the quality of your success. These are efficiency tools, meant to help make life more streamlined so you can focus on producing. What we have seen is the reliance on technology for our productivity, but the ignorance of building our own capacity first.

You could build a house in a couple days; people are probably trying. This is not a statement of productivity; this is a statement of speed, quickness, and efficiency. Today we are completing more and more, and organizations are getting a lot of things done. But we are not doing it with the utmost quality we could have, or productivity that we should require from ourselves.

If life were perfect, this book wouldn't matter that much. Imagine if life were like that game where you must organize the shapes to fit into a square box. It's easy when you remove the pieces one by one and know exactly which piece goes where. But the game is impossible or feels impossible when you get one of those pieces in the wrong spot; the constraints of the size limit your ability to change course or pivot while you are doing it. This is life: It is easy when the pieces fall into place, and the reality is that you really don't have to grow or change much when everything fits perfectly. As you already know, we are becoming more and more restrictive in our life because of the demands we have. Up until this point many people have learned only to prioritize or manage their puzzle pieces. **But we are telling you there is a different way, a better way. We want to show you how much easier it is if you have 10 different ways and a lot more room to fit each piece. That is what building your capacity does: It allows you to grow to make the right move; it allows you to be resilient to whatever curve ball comes your way. You can build your foundation so strong that when you need it you have the range to go right, left, up, or down.**

We are on a mission to help 10 million people build their capacity, because a world where people reach their true potential is in our opinion what true abundance is meant to look like.

How do you measure your organization's capacity?

Capacity Index

There are three key metrics that when combined evaluate how much capacity your organization has.

1. **Engagement:** There are equations that evaluate how much cost and productivity an engaged employee has verses a disengaged employee.
2. **Health-Care Costs:** There is no denying that a healthy employee is a better employee. When you have employees that are heavily medicated, are overweight, and have chronic medical conditions, it doesn't only impact your bottom line; it also impacts their performance.
3. **Profitability:** We understand that not all organizations are for profit, but this is the best connector for evaluating capacity. If there is room to improve engagement and decrease health-care costs, it is certain that you are missing out on profits.

Look at a sample of what happens when your people have more *capacity*. These numbers come from the same organization:

Employees: 5,000
Revenue: $6 billion

Limited Capacity
Engagement Level: 28 percent
Health-Care Costs: $12,000/per employee ($60 million)
Profitability: 32 percent

Expanded Capacity
Engagement Level: 35 percent
Health-Care Costs: $9,600/per employee ($48 million)
Profitability 37 percent

Summary: Key Points

Chapter 1

Capacity is your ability to *do more*, *have more*, and *give more*. This is your container; imagine if you had more room!

Chapter 2

All organizations are *people with a purpose*. You must build your most valuable assets' most valuable asset: their health.

Chapter 3

Five Problems
1. Demands are increasing and capacity is shrinking.
2. Stress is melting us down.
3. We overrely on skills and talent.
4. Engagement is lousy.
5. Our health is embarrassing.

Chapter 4

Human capital is the foundation to the future and it always will be. You can't run a ship without a crew!

Chapter 5

Focus is a skill; it is the most valuable skill because it is what directs performance. Just because you can't focus now doesn't mean you don't have the ability to later. *Practice* this skill; it guides everything else in your life.

Chapter 6

Energy is your most precious commodity. Energy is the fuel to performance. We want you to build your energy, we want you to protect your energy, and most importantly, we want you to share your energy.

energy + passion = *drive*

Chapter 7

Drive is your internal motivation to succeed and is the propeller to life.

Chapter 8

We all will have stress. Most of it we can control with our thoughts, but even so, the real solution to stress is to implement more thoughtful rest on a weekly, daily, or hourly basis.

Chapter 9

Does your current nutrition plan support the three On Target Living principles? For a full understanding of these principles. Please visit: http://ontargetliving.com/3-principles/.

Three Principles:
1. Cell health
2. pH balance
3. Source

Chapter 10

Exercise is great, but *movement* is essential. Think about moving your body daily.

Chapter 11

If you see a problem and you know the solution, you have the *power* to change anything!

Acknowledgments

From Chris

There are so many people who have helped and inspired me along my journey that I would like to thank. I'd like to begin with many of my teachers: To Miss Ellis, my sixth-grade teacher, who told me that I could be whoever I wanted to be. To a few of my college professors—Dr. Louis Junker, who opened my eyes to a world of better health, and to Dr. Kwok Ho, who pulled me into the prevention arena.

To my dad, who taught me how to laugh and listen, and to my mother, who taught me to be kind—thank you for all your love and support.

To our faithful On Target Living clients, readers, and followers, whose phone calls, letters, e-mails, and testimonials drive me to learn and grow every day—thank you!

To our wonderful team at On Target Living—Dawn, Mark, Kristen, Tab, Barry, Matt, Lisa, Patrick, and Anthony—you are changing lives.

To the friends and family who have supported me from the beginning—thank you!

To my two biggest cheerleaders, Dawn Miller and my daughter, Kristen—thank you for the positive sunshine you bring to me and the rest of our world each day; you are a gift.

To my son, Matt, who drove this project from the beginning—you have grown into a great leader, but more importantly, a terrific father and friend.

To my little girl, Dolly—your love changed me.

Finally, to the rock in my world, my wife, Paula—thank you for all your love and support; our journey together keeps getting better!

From Matt

Have you ever wondered what impact you have made on a person's life? We have found that there are hundreds of people in our lives that have made positive impacts, and they don't even know it. This is our chance to say thank you! Because without them, this book wouldn't be possible.

> Barry Napier—thanks for simplifying the vision.
> Patrick McGinn—you have a beautiful way with words.
> Pete Gaughan—thanks for the coaching.
> Lisa Prang—you made this book more than words.
> OTL Team—Dawn, Mark, Kristen, Paula, Tab, Anthony—thanks for all of your support.
> Mr. Mac, my high school golf coach—you taught me sports were more than performance; they were about honesty, integrity, and teamwork. You were the most positive coach I have ever had. Love you to this day!
> Don Underwood, my college golf coach—we did not always see eye to eye, but your positive impact will always be remembered. You always believed in me, when at times it would have been easier to give up. Thanks, Don!
> All my friends, family, mentors, and coworkers who have always supported me, especially my biggest cheerleader, my twin sister Kristen. My amazing mother, Paula Johnson, you gave me the work ethic and tenacity to get things done! My mentor, boss, co-author, and best friend, Chris Johnson, you

have always been my role model and I am lucky to work with you everyday.

My wife and best friend, Holly, you make me so happy!

Last, to Boji and LJ, and to my son, Eze. I can't wait to watch you grow.

Index